The Gigging Musician

The Gigging Musician

How to Get, Play, and Keep the Gig

by Billy Mitchell

Backbeat
Books

San Francisco

Published by Backbeat Books
600 Harrison Street
San Francisco, CA 94107
An imprint of the Music Player Network
United Entertainment Media, Inc.
Publishers of *Gigging* magazine and MusicPlayer.com

Distributed to the book trade in the U.S and Canada by
Publisher's Group West, 1700 Fourth Street, Berkeley, CA 94710

Distributed to the music trade in the U.S. and Canada by
Hal Leonard Publishing, P.O. Box 13819, Milwaukee, WI 53213

Cover Design: Peter Holwitz
Cover Composition: Greene Design
Text Design and Composition: Nancy Tabor

Library of Congress Cataloging-in-Publication Data:
Mitchell, Billy
    The gigging musician: how to get, play, and keep the gig /
by Billy Mitchell; foreword by Bill Evans
        p. cm.
    Includes index
    ISBN: 0-87930-634-3 (alk. paper)
    1. Popular music—Vocational guidance. 2. Music trade. I. Title

ML3795. M53 2000
780'.68—dc21   00-052779

Printed in the United States of America

01 02 03 05 05 06   6 5 4 3 2 1

Table of Contents

Chapter 4: Women on the Road   25

How far have women come since the early days? Gaining a better understanding of where we are by checking out where we've been.

Interviews:

Chapter 5: Thinking 24–7   45

Planning ahead is a key to success. Knowing what your day and gig will be, and that all loose ends are taken care of, alleviates stress.

Interview: Gregg Field   48
    (Grammy-nominated drummer/producer)

Part 1 Conclusion   53

Part 2—Your Band:
Relating to Other Musicians   55

. . . .

Chapter 6: Split Personalities,   57
or the Eight Faces of a Bandleader

In the music business, you deal with an array of personalities, especially those responsible for leading. If you've played in a band, you've met one or been one.

Chapter 7: The Big "Mo"   69

In order to move a band forward, everyone must have a positive attitude and be willing to do what has to be done.

Chapter 8: Understand, Understanding . . . Understood?   75

In order for a group to survive, it should have definition. Who is responsible for what? How do things get done?

Part 2 Conclusion   87

Part 3—Your Gig:
Taking Care of the Business of Music   89

• •

Chapter 9: What Would "Bird" Say?   91

The drug culture has always been a part of the music scene, affecting every individual's performance and spirituality.

Chapter 10: Conversation Over!   99

On the way up, it's just as important to treat your finances as well as you should treat people.

Acknowledgements

This book is dedicated to Bessie Mitchell (1902-) and all the people who have helped me on my way. A special thanks to the Pedrini family (Pedrini Music, Alhambra, CA), and all the great musicians who helped me survive and grow in the business. To Bill Evans and *Gig* magazine for giving me the opportunity to share my soul in hopes of helping others on their way. A special thanks to Samantha Laine, and "Bliss," at *Gig* for their editorial assistance, and Albert Hernandez and Bob Gerholdt of Copy Graphics for their patience and generosity.

Foreword

· · · · · · · · · · · · · · · · · · · ·

I first met Billy Mitchell a half-dozen years ago when I was a local newspaper editor who gigged on the side and he was a local gigger who did a bit of writing on the side. In fact, it was some of his writing for the *L.A. Jazz Scene* that helped plant the seed for *level11mag.com,* the website I worked on that led directly to the relaunch of *Gig Magazine.* Fittingly, Billy is the only writer on the *Gig* team whose work has appeared in every issue.

Billy is—for lack of a better term—*Gig's* philosopher king. His column is by far the most read and commented on part of the magazine. When we were first approached to do books based on the *Gig* ethos, Billy's column was a natural starting point. But this book is more than just a compendium of past columns. Billy has gone back and expanded on some of his original submissions and added interviews with A-list players and business types, to give some added perspective.

You will find this book divided into three parts: "You," "Your Band," and "Your Gig." These deal with personal issues that affect all performing musicians at one time or another, interpersonal issues that will crop up regardless of whether they have a 10-piece band or are solo artists, and straight business and professional issues that every gigger has to face. You will also find, at the end of each section, some "real-life" ideas, questions, and exercises intended to help put some of Billy's concepts into practice.

There are a few folks to acknowledge who have been instrumental in the survival and success of *Gig* in its formative years. Although many of them have moved on to other pursuits, without their passion and support, there would be no *Gig* and likely no book. My undying thanks to Paul Gallo, Herb Schiff, Quint Randle, Hector LaTorre, Marty Porter, Riva Danzig, Diane Gershuny, Joy Zaccaria, Andy Myers, Albert Margolis, and John Hurley. Thanks also to my wife, Linda, and my daughter, Erin, for their love and support and for putting up with the kind of schedule it takes to put together a magazine every month. (I promise I'll take a vacation soon. No, really.)

Finally, thanks to Billy Mitchell, for his integrity, honesty, and wisdom. I hope you learn as much from him as I have.

Bill Evans
Editor-in-Chief
Gig Magazine

Introduction
(About the Author)

My experience in music might strike some people as a tad unconventional. I seem to have entered the music business backwards. As a child I was exposed to music in my home (my mother taught piano) and I showed a strong inclination toward playing the piano. But I also had a serious aversion to the discipline needed to develop in music. Playing was fun—practice was not. I was a typical triple-A personality and preferred cowboys and Indians, and later sports and chicks, to spending countless hours practicing a musical instrument. I certainly did not expect to end up in the music business. But, as is true of many mothers, my mother had the gift of prophecy. Her words have remained with me as a haunting reminder: She told me constantly that music was a part of me and that I would "practice now . . . or practice later."

Later for me came toward the end of the 1980s, after many years as a performer and several successful albums. Some people (those who didn't scrutinize me too closely) regarded me as a fairly good player. But it didn't take long to notice my deficiencies—problems that never would have existed had I listened to Mama. To compensate for these shortages, I developed in other areas—production, promotion, organization, and, arguably, people skills—all those things that help a musician "put it together." On the way I supported a family by holding several jobs—salesman, record promoter, investigator, school teacher—that allowed me to interact with people and learn in different areas. All the while, I remained active as a performer, trying to keep a day job and play music at night, doing neither one particularly well. It was not until the '90s, after establishing a bit of a reputation as a producer and bandleader, that I decided to make music the focus of my life. This could be considered getting into the music business backwards.

Many changes were taking place in the business. And, although I was fortunate to be able to work with and learn from many great artists, I began to recognize various inconsistencies. Often, good musicians who were much more qualified and dedicated than I didn't work as much as I did. I thought this curious, if not unfair. Where was the justice in our creative universe? I noticed how quickly the disillusionment and frustration experienced by young musicians, as they struggled to make sense out of the nonsensical, turned into anger and burnout. Why? What makes the music business different? As time passed, I noticed that my brethren had problems with what I considered commonsense issues.

I believe this is because our educational system focuses on theory and leaves the "driving" to life. In other words, "You're on your own." Schools don't deal with survival issues because most teachers are smart enough to come off of the road early and settle for a life in academia. They also know that only the strong will survive, ultimately. I suppose teachers don't want the responsibility of discouraging the half-hearted . . . the *business* will do that.

This book is my effort to help bridge some of the gaps that interfere with making progress in the music business. I see very little difference in the problems that musicians face and those we all face in everyday life. The music business is intense, but no more intense than, say, Wall Street. The stakes are as high as the risks. And you may find yourself in competition with someone who, in reality, should not be on the same stage. I believe that it is as important for an artist to know what to expect as it is to know what to do. We somehow come to believe that if we do A, B, and C, then D, E, and F will happen. This logic may apply if you've received a law degree from Harvard or a doctorate from M.I.T., but it has little to do with life after Juilliard.

I've seen countless books on theory and principles but very few on problem solving. Although this is not exactly a "how to" book, I think that much can be learned by checking out some of the experiences, philosophies, and ideas of those who've made it in the field. I realized from the beginning that in order to make this book comprehensive, it would have to include much more than my highly emotional, sometimes unqualified opinions. And so I called on people who were active in the business. People who have contributed to and affected various areas of the business, all from different backgrounds, but all willing to give of themselves in order to make it easier for others. For that I am most thankful. This information gave this project a life of its own—good, honest information that will allow us to learn from the ancient tradition called "word of mouth." This means we are learning from those who have already experienced both the setbacks and the successes of the business. And as this project developed, I came to realize that if I had had this insight at the beginning of my career, I might have been a much better musician, a better leader, even a better person.

This book is a compilation of my "Road Warrior" articles, featured monthly in *Gig Magazine,* including the accompanying interviews with individuals who have worked in various areas of the music business. This is intended to provide insight into the music world by analyzing the attitudes, philosophies, and experiences of those who have made it their careers. Because of the subjective nature of art and music, I feel safe in saying that there can be no one way of looking at anything. Rather, by studying varying experiences, we make varying applications, thus drawing conclusions. We will learn that there are many ways to look at issues as an artist. I hope this book will help you formulate an approach to this business of music that will be most beneficial for you. By presenting an array of mini-bios, we hope to expose you to multiple perspectives and thereby enable you to explore the different sides of every issue.

We study causality as we discuss what to do, as well as what not to do. We deal with such principles as:

- If you don't do nothin', nothin's going to happen.

- If you keep on doing the same stupid things, you can expect the same stupid results.

- Do *something* . . . even if it's wrong.

- Your present situation is most likely the result of the things you've done, or haven't done.

- If someone has a hard time making it, there's usually a reason.

Although these statements may seem a little harsh, they are part of life's realities, realities that are magnified for those who choose to enter the music business.

PART 1

·······························

YOU

Dealing with Personal Issues

While this is not some kind of psychobabble self-help book, it is difficult, if not impossible, to get your gig together unless you have yourself together first. This can mean anything from personal habits that impede your performance to dealing with the fear of the rejection that is a standard part of playing music for a living.

—Bill Evans

In Chapter 4 ("Women on the Road") you will find a discussion of some specific issues that confront female giggers.

You may find that some of the personal issues covered in Part 1 don't apply to you at all and that others hit uncomfortably close to home. Those latter issues, brothers and sisters, are the ones to begin working on.

Chapter 1

······················

No Fear

"There is nothing to fear but fear itself." Who said
that? It certainly was not I. For many years as a performing
artist, I must admit, there were many aspects of the music
business and the gig that frightened me to death. Although
fear may be an integral part of human nature, it must be con-
trolled like any other emotion. A musician must turn the natural flow of adrenaline into a creative force and transform nervous energy into "persona power."

One type of fear that grips all artists is the fear of rejection.
No one enjoys being turned down for anything. But often
rejection has nothing to do with you as a musician. When a
record label turns down your material, it does not necessarily
mean they don't like your songs. Most likely it means their roster is full, and they don't have the means to properly handle
your project. They may have an artist who is similar in style or
may not have any experience with the market for your type of
music.

There are countless reasons groups are turned down that
have absolutely nothing to do with their music. The debilitat-

ing side of this fear of rejection is that it can be paralyzing and stop your career cold. To avoid rejection, musicians may just do nothing. They fail to complete songs and projects, because they fear their work may be rejected. Or they do too much, to avoid finishing their work. They continue to make changes and rewrites, or keep upgrading equipment and never complete a particular project to offer up for public approval—or rejection. I was spared that particular dilemma early on because I cared little about what people felt about my music. I just did it, and I still just do it. And if somebody likes it, all the mo' better!

But I did suffer deep anxiety when it came to other issues: my instrument, other musicians, and the audience. Down through the years, I've learned how unfounded my fears were, and I've been able to turn my fear into fun. It took a lot of introspection and an honest evaluation of purpose. But I've finally learned how to avoid being intimidated by my instrument, by musicians, or by the audience.

The fact is, if you don't thoroughly prepare yourself to play your chosen instrument, it's going to kick your butt every time you pick it up. Only through practice will you find comfort in knowing that you are prepared for whatever happens. You have to practice "past the gig." If your band does blues in three keys, practice the blues in five keys. If you are playing with a singer, try to learn the lyrics as well as the chart. Practice past the gig so you don't sit in fear that your band will try out music you're not familiar with, or worry that you don't have the chops to handle it.

As I began to take my practicing seriously, I found myself becoming more comfortable around other musicians. Being afraid of our peers is a malady suffered by most of us. As soon as other musicians show up at our gig, our playing changes as well as our attitude. It's as if we musicians have to prove our ability when in the company of our peers instead of concentrating on the job we're being paid to do.

I recently dropped in on a wedding reception where some friends were playing. When they saw me walk in, it went from a classy little reception to the Newport Jazz Festival. Why? Nobody at the function was interested in how many chops these musicians had. Those people were celebrating a wedding. It took me a long time to realize that nothing should alter my performance. I do what I do. I am not paid to impress fellow players. I am paid to do the gig.

Some of us never overcome our fear of crowds, especially when the crowd's attention is focused on us. Being nervous before a performance is natural—even healthy! It gives us that edge that helps us focus and dig down within ourselves. But when the audience is intimidating to a performer, there is a problem. All the fear boils up and the audience becomes our enemy instead of our support. Our anxiety crescendos as we perceive negatives being directed toward ourselves and our music. And we are usually wrong!

One of the great learning experiences of my career came during a club engagement at Birdland in New York. I was playing my heart out while scanning the audience for a reaction. One lady in particular caught my attention. Sitting right in front of me, she glared at me through the whole set. She never smiled, clapped, tapped her feet, or anything. I began to think she hated me. But why? My music couldn't be that bad. Did I remind her of her ex-husband? Was this someone from my past whom I'd forgotten? Was she going to kill me when I came off the stage? And the fear grew as the set continued and she continued to just stare. The set ended and, in a show of internal bravado, I passed as close to the lady's table as I could.

As I neared her, she reached out and grabbed my arm and said, "Young man, I haven't enjoyed piano like that in many years!" I was shocked! She continued, "I'm going to stay for the next set." I thanked her, and my life was changed.

From that time on, I stopped trying to second-guess the audience. I realized that people don't come out and spend their money to see us fail. They come out to hear a good performance and enjoy themselves. Fear can distort our perception of the audience and everything else. It can make us forget that the audience as well as our instrument and fellow musicians can be a source of enormous and gratifying support—not intimidation.

Stan
Behrens

Those who are not familiar with the name of Stan
Behrens have more than likely enjoyed his music. Stan's recent
credits include appearing as featured soloist on TV soundtracks
for *Renegade*, the new *Rockford Files*, and the feature film *Raw
Justice*. Other appearances include *Murder She Wrote*, *A Different
World*, *Bay Watch*, *Coach*, *Dr. Quinn Medicine Woman*, and
Deadline.

His harmonica and sax have accompanied such artists as
Alice Cooper, Jefferson Starship, jazz organist Jimmy Smith,
and blues greats Bo Diddley, Ruth Brown, and Chicago blues

master Willie Dixon. He has two solo albums to his credit: *Harmonica Deluxe* and *The Stan Behrens—Willie Dixon Project*. As a working musician he never fails to deliver good times with his blend of blues, jazz, R&B, and rock and roll.

BM: I always begin from the start so that I can better understand the present.
STAN: I began playing music when I was a little kid. I learned easily because I could hear the music and I would just play along. I got good at that . . . to a certain point. There's only so far you can go, there's only so much you can teach yourself before you have to reach out and look to other people to show you things.

BM: How did you teach yourself?
STAN: Just listening to records, and going to see other people play. I always tried to emulate the things that I liked.

BM: Were you concerned about theory and scales and all of that?
STAN: I had no concept at all. I couldn't make a C chord. I would hear something and pick up my instrument and imitate it. I always got encouragement from some of the really great players. I was even told that I played so good that I didn't have to learn how to read and write. And I kinda went along with that. . . for a while.

And also, I was into the blues and I was emulating blues guys. They always had hard, troubled lives, and I sort of fell into that bag too. You idolize somebody who ain't makin' it . . . but they have very colorful lives, I'd say. I kind of went along that way until one day I found myself being a lot like them. They were all poor and broke . . . good musicians, but couldn't make a good living at it.

I came out to California from New York with Ruth Brown. I had recorded some things in New York with Johnny Winter and Alice Cooper. They put me on their record but I never got any credit for it. I was young. I didn't know. It was kind of weird. I went into this Alice Cooper session and they said, "Hi! Why don't you come sit in on a session?" So I laid down a track . . . not thinking anything of it. Two weeks later I turn on the AM station and the guy goes, "Heeeeeere's Alice." I said, "Sh— ! That ain't Alice . . . that's *me*!'

BM: So that was another lesson.
STAN: That was another lesson. All of a sudden there I was bigger than anything. As soon as the record started there was that harmonica comin' right at you.

BM: Do you remember the name of the album?
STAN: Yeah! The album was called *Muscle of Love,* and the song was entitled "Working Up a Sweat." I have it here.

BM: And you never got a dime?
STAN: Not a dime . . . not even a mention on the record. I wasn't thinking about contracts. I was young and just didn't know any better.

But meanwhile I'm in L.A., and I've got this little buzz going.You know, the new, hot harmonica player in town. And I'm working with some of the Jazz heavies, like Jimmy Smith, on gigs where a lot of the recording industry people pass through. I started getting calls from Mike Post and other composers who were doing music for the TV shows. Which was great because a lot of those guys liked the way I played. So they would give me a space and have me play in it. Which was real cool 'cause as long as I didn't have to read anything I was fine.

But then one day I get this call from Mike Post. I think it was during the 1980 Olympics. They were doing this orchestral session. And he sits me there in the orchestra. There's a book and it says HARMONICA on the front of it. And I'm going, "Oooohhh noooooo."

I open up the book and the tune starts out with a harmonica solo . . . *written out!* They count off the tune and there are 50 studio musicians waiting on my first line. Everybody's looking at me and I'm petrified. Finally I said, "Mike, can we talk? Maybe I can overdub my part later." And Mike was real cool. He let me overdub the part. And I had to walk away from that scene with my tail between my legs. The musicians were asking, "Who's this guy? He can't play. What is he doing here?"

And I was getting other calls. And then I got a call from John Williams' people about coming to play at the Hollywood Bowl. They were doing "A Night at the Movies" and they had these movie themes that had harmonica in them. It scared me to death. I actually told them that I couldn't do it. It scared me so badly that I turned it down.

BM: Was that enough to get you into reading?

STAN: Well, a couple of those experiences came by where all of a sudden there was this opportunity for me to be something in the recording industry . . . and I couldn't. I sat down with myself and had to admit that there was a lot of important stuff that I just didn't know. So I went and I enrolled in college. I studied the whole tonal system and began working on my reading . . . which was really weird, because I studied all this theory, which helped me to write, but I still had a hard time reading. I always seemed to have a mental block. So what I do now is twice a week I go over to West LA College and I sit and play saxophone charts with the big band. And now I read so much better. Just within this past year I've made this giant leap. It helps me that much more with everything else, because once I could read it I could play it on any instrument.

BM: So what would you say to the young guys who are coming up?

STAN: I would say to all you young people who have aspirations of being a musician and taking your craft all the way, you have to get the education, with a real stress on reading. Another thing I found out: If you know how to read, all kinds of doors open up. You can play so many more things. You don't have to sit there and try to learn a song. You can just open up a book and play it . . . just like that! You don't have to sit there wearing out your tapes trying to learn a solo. If it's written out you play it . . . just like that!

Chapter 2

....

Culture Clash

If you are a traveling musician, you may have noticed different cultures that make up the American landscape. For that matter, there probably are enough variations to qualify the United States as several distinct countries in one. Each area has its own customs and social patterns that make it unique. As musicians, we are used to carrying ourselves in a relaxed, informal manner, seldom aware of the customs and politics of the places we visit, and usually we're not interested. But as musicians, we are often unknowing ambassadors of goodwill. We are usually observed and scrutinized a lot more closely than the average tourist.

It is particularly important for you as a musician to be aware of your environment, for a number of reasons. One is that your survival may depend upon it. But most importantly, the people you come in contact with will appreciate you more when they know that you've not only taken the time to learn about them but that you respect their local culture.

There are many do's and don'ts that vary from place to place. For example, a visitor from Iowa in Los Angeles for the first time may think that flashing the peace sign at a group of teenagers would signify friendship when, in fact, that gesture could be misconstrued as a gang sign—which, in turn, would result in a buttful of bullets. It is interesting how the most innocent gestures or comments could have such different results, depending on where and how they are expressed. So it is important for all traveling musicians to know what each gesture means in the area of the world they're visiting. If you are not sure, it is best to keep your hands to yourselves.

There is a whole series of cross-cultural communications that as traveling musicians we should be aware of. It is as much a part of our expression in relating to others as our music is. We never think of these antics because they are a natural part of our behavior. Rarely do we realize the differences that simple gestures make around the world. As working musicians we're exposed to different situations on a continuing basis. So it is important that we know where we're going and how to conduct ourselves when we get there. There are greetings, farewells, hand signs, touching, hugging, and kissing customs, facial expressions and body language that mean one thing here and something entirely different over there.

In my travels, I have learned many lessons in diversity—some the hard way, but they were lessons nonetheless. Musicians almost always have cameras, especially when traveling internationally. It is important to document your travels and your gigs. But you have to be aware you cannot just be snapping pix because you see something nice. It could put you in jeopardy, as it did me on a recent visit to Sao Paulo, Brazil. While on an afternoon stroll, I passed by a very old building that I thought would make a wonderful snapshot. I didn't really notice the two rather attractive women caught in the lower left of the frame. However, they noticed me and approached, shouting and gesturing for me to stop. One pulled out a badge. I didn't notice if it was police or military, but I knew it was legit! As I attempted to calm them down, a passerby noticed that I spoke no Portuguese, intervened on my behalf, and explained to them that I was a tourist. That stranger probably kept me from going to jail over just a simple snapshot. I've been aware ever since that, if you want to take pictures of people these days, you'd best ask their permission. You may unknowingly snap someone on the run or someone who holds the belief that a photo steals part of the soul. Any one of these scenarios spells the blues.

Then you have codes of conduct. When I went to Japan, I experienced a lesson in civility for the first time. After walking around the city of Osaka for a few hours, I noticed that I had not made real eye contact with anyone. I realized that it must have been obvious that I was the only African American brother within miles—which would draw stares even in parts of the United States. Yet no one stared at me. The beauty of it is in their philosophy: It is impolite to stare or make lingering eye contact. Their custom is just the opposite of the direct eye-to-eye contact we are taught in America. Shortly after that, I arrived in the Middle East—talk about culture shock! The first thing my band was instructed was not to talk about politics with anyone, not to stare, and not even to look at any of the native women. As you can imagine, that took some getting used to. But we handled it.

Being a musician allows you to visit places you probably could not afford to see as a run-of-the-mill traveler. It is good to analyze the customs around the world and understand how they came to be. Knowing what your performing environment is about will only enhance your performance. The variations of culture should not be a distraction or an irritation. They should be an inspiration and a part of your overall learning experience. After all, that's what music is about. That's what life is about.

Joe Sample

Joe Sample began his professional career with the
Jazz Crusaders. But since launching his solo career, in the late
1970s, he has become one of the most enduring artists of the
contemporary jazz scene. He has recorded with a cross section
of music greats and continues to tour internationally with his
own group. As a Warner Brothers recording artist he has
received several Grammy nominations and consistently tops
the recording industry music charts.

BM: I've been a fan of yours since before I started playing. We
used to sneak into clubs in New York, when the legal age was
18, to see you play when you were with the Jazz Crusaders. I
don't think you were too much older. If anyone has had road
experience it would be you.

JS: When I began in music I knew there would be a lot of traveling. I didn't know it would become what it has today. As a
musician I've seen a lot of changes over the last 40 years. I
began recording and touring with the Crusaders around 1963.
So I've been on the road for the last 37 years. When we started
touring from coast to coast, you would pass various band
buses going up and down Route 66. The buses at that time
were set up like regular Greyhound buses . . . very uncomfortable. Travel in the old days was brutal. If you traveled like we
did, mostly by van, it was a nightmare. We didn't have the

Joe Sample and Billy Mitchell.

money to buy anything bigger. Today the buses have changed. They're set up like somebody's living room now and provide a better "on the road" life style. There was no sanity. You had to be a very strong-willed person with a lot of tolerance for pain. You had to be proud of the band you were playing with and have a profound love of the music and performing. Not only was the travel hard, but you had to deal with terrible equipment in the clubs. Sometimes the pianos were atrocious.

BM: I have a chapter about traveling through different countries and experiencing various customs. Has that ever created any challenges for you?

JS: When you go into a foreign country, the first thing you have to realize is that you have left your homeland, and you are entering a place where these people have had a society of their own for thousands of years. And they have a culture. They have customs, cuisine, and styles of their own. The musi-

cian should go with the intention of celebrating this new culture that he/she has been invited to participate in. You should
never go anywhere being angry and mad because the place
doesn't resemble the culture that you just left. That is the
dumbest thing that I've witnessed.

I've seen musicians get upset because . . . in many countries
the water is not the same, and they demand "real water," "bot-
tled water," and it's just not available. They don't understand
that not only are the people different, even the minerals in the
ground are different. They didn't find gold in France. They had
the California gold rush. That's what is so beautiful about the
world . . . it has so many different things to offer. Don't get
caught up in what you're accustomed to. Open your mind!
Once you've done that, it will be open about a lot of things.

You can go from one city to another, right here in this
country, and thing change drastically. You have to open your
mind up and accept where you are. When you're traveling with
a group of musicians who have wide-open minds, always looking for the best in everything, who will give their best performance no matter what the conditions are, you are going to have
an incredibly wonderful time. I remember I toured with a band
called The Soul Committee. We had so much fun musically
and spiritually that when the tour ended, we didn't want to
come home.

BM: Was that because of how you were received, or because
you were grooving together?

JS: Being received is a result of how we interact with each
other. We have to create the acceptance. We enjoyed each other
so much, and you could feel it in the music. If we're having
fun, we draw the audience, pull them in, invite them into that
wonderful world that we have created. This is the power of performance, the magic of music.

Chapter 3

·······························

The Thin Line Between Persistence and Being a Pain in the Ass

One of my major concerns is the lack of preparation young artists receive before entering the entertainment arena. A tremendous amount of fine talent is destroyed before it can even develop, due to the convoluted and frequently misunderstood nature of the music business. Young artists seldom know the difference between music as an art form and music as a money-making venture. We mislead our young musicians into thinking that by doing A, B, and C they may then expect X, Y, and Z to follow. Such is not the case.

I received a letter from D. R., an award winning songwriter from Fort Smith, Arkansas. D. R. has experienced some curious turnarounds from publishers to whom he has pitched his tunes. He says he receives very positive responses initially, but then, for some unknown reason, the communication lines close down and the prospective deals fade. In response to D. R.'s letter, I'd like to focus on two attributes many musicians, including myself, often have difficulty with: patience and a sense of balance.

19

If someone changes on you for no apparent reason, you may be dealing with a knucklehead. If the same scenario plays out two or three times with other contacts, you may be dealing with coincidence. If you find yourself on the receiving end of a complete shift in response and attitude for a fourth time, you'd best start checking yourself. Chances are you're doing a good job of pissing everyone off with your aggressive behavior. In the music business, a very thin line exists between persistence and aggravation. Follow-up is important. But if you establish yourself as someone who calls the publisher, the club, the agent every day to see "what's happening," you establish yourself as someone few people want to deal with.

It's important to understand that when you pitch a song, a group, or a track, you are a salesperson, not a musician. You have to let the prospective buyer know not only that your music is cool, but also that *you* are cool, someone with whom it would be a pleasure to work. Know this: Companies aren't looking for tunes; they have more material than they can place. Realistically—unless you're in Nashville—publishers do very little to get songs placed. Tin Pan Alley is a thing of the past. If you want to move tunes quickly, you need to hook up with producers with projects and active recording artists looking for tunes.

It is crucial that you keep one thing real clear: You are the only one who realizes the full potential of your work. Though your family and friends may praise your material, it will probably not have the same effect on a detached listener who hears floodtides of music day in and day out. These hit (money) mavens can't hear what you hear. As a matter of fact, they sometimes can't hear anything. For that very reason, many hits are often tunes previously rejected or passed over, added to an album as filler or an afterthought. Were there just one group that could accurately forecast hits, the dynamics of the music business would change drastically.

So to answer D. R.: I encourage you to exercise patience. Give publishers time. Give them a week or two before you follow up. If it's not happening, thank them for their time and tell them you'll check back in a few weeks. Move on to the next contact. You can't force your music on anyone, but you can become a pain in the ass.

These people know what they need. If they hear your material at the right moment, remember you as a cool person, and hear something they're looking for, they'll get in touch with you. Just keep doing what you're supposed to do. It may be a matter of weeks, months, or even years, but things do come back around when you put your work and yourself out there in a professional, confident manner.

Darlene Chan

Darlene Chan began her career while a student at the University of California at Berkeley, producing the first three UC Jazz Festivals. She joined Festival Productions in 1969 and is now director of the West Coast office. She currently produces major music festivals, including Playboy, JVC, and Benson & Hedges, as well as award-winning TV presentations. She recently received the Founders Award for her contributions to the music community.

BM: I know that as a festival producer you must get bombarded with all kinds of packages and presentations. What turns you off the most?

DC: I think that one of the worst things someone could do is to be rude to my staff. Often, we are so busy that artists may have a difficult time speaking directly with me, and they end up speaking to someone on my staff. If you have an attitude with them because you can't speak to me, that turns me off right away. Our MO here is not to be rude to anyone, so I support my people all the way.

Another thing is when someone implies that we're "out to get them," just because I'm not able to book them. If I'm not going to use an act, I try to express that in the nicest way that I know how. And there are many reasons. Sometimes the group just doesn't fit the venue, or maybe we just don't like the music.

I have managers calling me continually, and as long as they're polite, I don't mind, because that's their job. But once I've made it clear that this won't work, and they continue to call, it kind of gets to me. First of all it's time consuming. I just don't have the time to take every call. I totally understand it from the other side. If you're trying to promote someone that you totally believe in, and the person you're talking to just doesn't get it, it's frustrating. And sometimes we just flatly say no. But it's hard. Still, I don't think I've ever had anyone that turned me off so much that I wouldn't even listen to the tape.

BM: What do you think about the new generation of musicians?

DC: I get frustrated when I run into young musicians who happen to be talented and they've already copped an attitude by age 15. I don't justify anyone having an attitude at 35 either, but at least they've had time to work on it. We have a lot of young musicians who have what to me is a lack of respect. They have a lack of respect for the venue, for people, for other musicians. They have been told that they are great because they've made one of these all-star groups. And it seems that some of them think that they don't have to follow the rules. Again, the majority of them are fine . . . I'm hoping.

BM: Well, whose responsibility is that?

DC: It's about the parents and teachers. I don't think a music teacher needs to be a baby-sitter, but I think that music teachers need to drill into their students the importance of having respect for the *whole process* of being a musician.

BM: Do you think that this is a generational thing?

DC: I hope not. But it might be.

BM: It wasn't like that years ago, I don't think.

DC: Some youngsters seem to have adopted a "hot shot" type attitude that makes them believe they should be in the limelight.

BM: How do we correct this?

DC: I think it helps to have older musicians, who have been around, to come in and talk to them. More input from older musicians, mentoring . . . in a positive way. Many of the older musicians can tell the youngsters, firsthand, how these attitudes *did not* help them along the way. And then maybe some would say that you do need these attitudes to become successful, that you have to push or whatever. But one thing is for sure: It turns a lot of people that you have to do business with *off.*

Chapter 4

Women on the Road

I was involved in a spirited discussion about the role of women in this society. The point I was trying to make was that "they *have come* a long way." And although there has been much headway made by women in the music business, "they've still got a long way to go, baby." This chapter is about attitudes, primarily my own. Although I consider myself a progressive, "renaissance man" type, a real honest look into my own attitudes reveals some pretty interesting things. The question is: Do the guys accept their female counterparts as their equals, or only as gimmicks to enhance the stage presentation?

Historically, women have been limited to being singers and occasionally piano players. Not that women didn't stand out on other instruments or as leaders, but this was the exception. Often the singer would have to align herself personally with someone in the band in order to avoid creating interpersonal conflicts on the gig. They would have to develop a strong persona just to survive the rigors of the road. In days past, musicians and others in the arts were not held in the same regard that some are today, at least the ones that become successful.

There were definite boundaries that were not to be crossed. You must remember that during this part of our history women were strongly discouraged from entering medicine, law, the military, and all the areas traditionally reserved for men only. Women were just beginning to exercise their right to vote. There were exceptions, but this was pretty much the scene.

In music we labored under many myths. Beside the feminine nature's not being suited to the pressures of the road, women "were just not strong enough to play certain instruments" and "did not have the lung capacity to play certain horns." Those of you who would take issue with this should remember that this era also harbored other myths that were used to eliminate other minorities. Myths such as "Certain minorities could not sing opera or dance classically because their vocal chords and body structure would not allow it." And so, women, like other minorities, have been making a slow and tedious advance in this business. Only the boldly independent females have been able to overcome all the crap that this male-dominated business has subjected them to.

During the discussion I remembered that I had worked with a female bass player in the early 1970s, long before it became "hip." Her name was Tammy Burdett, and I believe she lives in Seattle now. I only knew of one other female bass player on the Los Angeles scene at the time. Her name was Carole Kaye, and she did a lot of the studio work around town. When we first started working together I guess it was kind of gimmicky. "Hey, look at this! A chick bass player." But soon I came not only to respect her ability and knowledge, but to depend on it.

Down through the years I have continued to work with female musicians from time to time. But I wonder just how much my mindset has matured. Am I really accepting female musicians as equals, or am I expecting them to enhance my band's appeal? I fear that somewhere back in the recesses of my little brain lie those old prejudices, those old myths. The fact that they can play equally as well as any man that I could hire for the job becomes secondary. Realizing this has given me pause for thought. I'm the one always talking about everything being equal. I don't suppose underlying reasons negate the actuality. You cannot turn on a network talk show or a late-night show without seeing women doing everything in the band, playing instruments that used to be a man's thing. I wonder about the motives. Are they as pure as we would like them to be? Have we truly moved to the next level of enlightenment? Or is it about what is most socially and politically correct? Or is it just about ratings?

I guess it ultimately doesn't matter why or how. It is only important that it *does* matter. Women have to be hired based on how they perform and nothing else. Women struggle for acceptance as police officers, firefighters, pilots, soldiers, and on and on. I guess it would be too much to expect that they would not have to struggle on the gig.

One's opinion about what women's role should be matters very little. It is no longer a matter of accepting. It is a matter of realizing that the scene has changed and women are an integral part of every aspect of it. The ladies have become proficient on every instrument made. You can argue if you like, but women on the gig are proving to be so much more than a visual. Just like in basketball, soccer, and other sports, women show more emotion, determination, dedication, commitment, and class than the fellas do. And the public is responding to it. If I ask you to find a drummer that can outswing, outfunk, or outplay Terri Lynn Carrington, I doubt you'll be able to do it!

Linda
Hopkins

Linda Hopkins is one of the most extraordinary
blues/gospel singers of this century. Born in New Orleans,
singing since the age of 3, inspired by Bessie Smith, and discov-
ered by Mahalia Jackson, Ms. Hopkins has entertained internationally for most of her 70+ years. She won a Tony Award and
a Drama Desk Award for *Inner City* and a second Tony Award
for creating the role of Bessie Smith in *Me and Bessie*, the
longest-running one-woman show on Broadway. She was featured on *The Tonight Show* with Johnny Carson a record 148
times and has released seven solo albums. She appeared in
Clint Eastwood's film *Honky Tonk Man* and in James Baldwin's
Go Tell It On the Mountain. In 1989 she was again nominated for
a Tony for the Broadway hit *Black and Blue*. Recent credits
include duets with B.B. King and tours with Branford Marsalis
and Albert Collins.

I never fail to mention that the time that I spent with "Miss
Linda" on the road was the greatest learning experience of my
life. She put me into musical situations that I had never experienced. And carried by the force of her incredible professionalism, I survived. I learned a lot about being a professional from
"Miss Linda" because this lady shared her knowledge unselfish-
ly. She is a truly incredible lady!

I inda Hopkins and Billy Mitchell (Paris 1989).

BM: Ms. Hopkins, I don't know of anyone who has had as long and as successful a career as you . . . and still going strong. I've always acknowledged that I learned more while working with you than in all my years working with other people put together. Women still face a lot of problems in the business. But it's important that people like you enable us to see where we have come from and the progress that has been made. What was it like when you first started singing and traveling with bands?

LH: Well, first of all, I learned from a lot of professional singers who took time to talk to me. They saw that I had potential and felt that I was a person that they could help. All of these big-name people—Billie Holiday, Ella Fitzgerald, Pearl

Bailey—sat me down and took time to tell me what this business was all about. I sat there and listened because I knew that they knew and I didn't. So my whole thing was to be obedient and humble and to hear what these people had to say. That's where I got my experience, from observing people and not taking anything upon myself.

BM: So you saw many of the problems that your mentors were experiencing firsthand.

LH: Billie Holiday sat me down and explained to me how she happened to get into this predicament with drugs and things. She said, "It's too late for me, but it's not too late for you." Anyone who comes up and offers you a cigarette, telling you that you need this, this will make you feel better, or something like that . . . you don't want nothing from nobody. That's how a lot of singers got hooked, taking stuff for sore throat and hoarseness and it turns out to be dope.

Pearl Bailey would tell me, "Honey, if you get a drink, and you set that drink down somewhere, don't come back and pick that drink up." And if someone takes a drink out of your glass, then give it to 'em because they could have something in their mouth. This is the way they get a lot of young people involved in drugs.

Ella Fitzgerald once told me that she never got involved in any of those things. She said, "I found out one thing, Linda. The people that give you all this stuff that turns your head, they're getting rich and keeping you poor." So you have to have sense enough to know that you can't be poor, and I can't make you rich. So you can't offer me anything!

Helen Humes gave me my first break in show business. She was the star of the show but she showed me how to be a headliner. Regardless of who you are on the bill with, no matter how great they sound, you don't need anything to boost you to go on out there. Take the strength of the person that was on before you. And know that what they did you can do better! I've never had to have a drink to keep myself going, and I've never smoked a cigarette or anything in my entire life. I kept myself strong because I was in show business. I'm an entertainer.

BM: You are a strong lady. When you perform on stage you look strong. I'm looking at you now, and you don't have a line on your face.

LH: I started in show business January 6, 1950. I just made 75 years old on December the 14th.

BM: What were some of the real hard things about working with bands and in clubs, years ago?

LH: I didn't have a lot of problems with too many musicians because most of them took me seriously. But there were always those bandleaders who felt that they could take liberties. And if you didn't want to get involved they would talk about you real bad. They would try to say that I wasn't a lady. You know! Not one musician can stand up and say that they had an affair with me. And then sometimes it was the women who would approach the men. So it worked both ways. In this business you have to be strong. You have to let it be known that you are all in the same business and "I don't go that way." If you're my boss, just let me work for you . . . and pay me, and let's be friends.

That's what I say to the young ladies. Go outside and get anything you want, but it should be outside of show business. Don't fool around with someone who already has someone at home. You're not hurting that other person as much as you're damaging your own self-respect. And I never lost respect for myself. That's why today everybody calls me "Mama Linda." That's the way everybody treated me because that's the way I conducted myself. Don't flirt around! Be a lady at all times, and that's the way you'll be treated.

BM: What about on the road? I'm trying to draw some comparisons between what bands went through then compared to now, with the social problems and such.

LH: I had kind of closed myself off from that because those were horrible times, mainly down South. We'd have to stay in hotels that were dirty. You'd have to clean them yourselves. You couldn't eat good food, we'd have to stop in grocery stores, and things. That's how I learned how to cook . . . on the road. Those were hurting days for me. Thank God they don't hurt anymore.

The people were hard on you then. They could be very mean to you. If they didn't like you or want to hear what you were doing, they would throw things at you. These are some of the things that we went through. I cried more than once on stage because of people. And then other audiences were very respectful. I remember working in Mississippi to a mixed audience. The whites were downstairs and the blacks were in the balcony. And you know, I got more respect from the white people. I took it that they were angry because they had to be upstairs. And I talked to them to let them know that I was singing to every individual in the place. But it was hard because I had to divide myself.

BM: Ms. Linda, you are a part of the history of American music. Your accomplishments down through the years . . . I know you've done *The Tonight Show* more than any other entertainer, just countless things that we could mention. I hope that your contribution to this project will help some of these young people develop a healthier approach to this business. People know and respect you all over the world. I've gone through customs with you in different countries, and they wouldn't even inspect our luggage. So they know you and trust you. What is your advice to prepare someone for handling success?

LH: Always be humble to people. Never get so big in show business that you can't sign an autograph or return fan mail. Take time to do these things. Without your audience you are nothing. And you are only as great as the audience receives you. You don't have to stand up and have conversations with everyone. Just be sweet, courteous, and humble. Be like a child to your public.

Ann
Patterson

Ann Patterson is best known as the leader of the highly acclaimed all-female big band Maiden Voyage, who have appeared internationally on TV and major festivals. She has backed, toured, or recorded with such artists as Joe Williams, Sheena Easton, Barry White, The Temptations, and Ray Charles, among others. As a music teacher she received the Vesta Award for outstanding achievement in the arts, and her profile has appeared in *American Women in Jazz, Women and Work,* and *Madame Jazz.*

BM: You're the leader of one of the swingin'est bands I've heard. Notice I didn't say female band. How did all that come together?

AP: Well, I started out as a classical oboe player, but I always had this secret dream of being a jazz saxophone player. I had gotten turned onto jazz at North Texas State College. But this was during the '60s, and you just didn't see women playing jazz in the big bands. So I didn't have any role models to encourage me. After getting a couple of degrees, I moved to L.A. and continued teaching. About this time the women's movement began to take off—we're talking about the '70s—and this gave me the confidence to try to become a jazz player.

BM: I think very few people realize how recent it has been that women began getting into the different areas and different instruments.

AP: The women that are coming up now, like the younger women that come into my band, it's no big deal to them. There were very few women from my generation playing jazz. There were some older women, because in the '40s they had a lot of all-girl bands. The men were off fighting the war, so somebody had to play the music back here.

BM: Just like the women's baseball league. And then, when it was over, it was over. So then in the '50s and '60s you have very few women playing jazz, maybe a few piano players.

AP: I was already classically trained. And inspired by the women's movement, I started studying sax and improvisation. In the beginning I signed up for band classes at the junior colleges. I couldn't get into any rehearsal bands, like at the union. Even when I was good enough, I met with the "women are only good for one thing" attitude on more than one occasion. Everyone didn't feel like that, but some did. Eventually, I worked my way into some rehearsal bands, one that was playing Don Ellis charts. When Don decided to put his band together, I was one of the players taken from the rehearsal band. That was a break for me because that visibility got me some other things.

In the early '80s I got involved with an all-girls situation. It didn't pan out for me, but I had the opportunity to meet some really good players. It gave me the idea that if there was a really strong all-female big band it might change some attitudes toward women musicians. I felt it might make it easier for us, because of the visibility, to get work in other bands. Also, it offered a safe environment for women musicians who wanted to play big band, to come and work out, develop their chops, network, and so forth.

BM: There must have been as many pluses as there were minuses.

AP: Maiden Voyage didn't meet with a lot of resistance, I think, because of the novelty of it. But we had to work very hard to get some of the major festivals that we began to get. We also got a lot of bookings because we were an all-female band. We also got a lot of support from some of the male musicians, who would give us clinics, charts, and all types of support.

I had more problems as a freelance musician than as the leader of an all-girls band, in the '80s especially. I rarely have a problem now. For example, on the casual scene there were certain casual leaders who, even being highly recommended, wouldn't call me because a female instrumentalist "just didn't look right." Another leader felt that the bride [at a wedding reception] might be a little uncomfortable having another woman "in the spotlight." I was hired to do a cruise ship in 1982, and when they found out I was a woman they canceled my contract. They claimed that it was about the band having to share a bathroom. I threatened to sue them. They hired me, and there was no problem. I remember being hired for a theatrical production with three other female musician/dancers, only to be offered one-third of what our male counterparts were offered. We refused and were replaced with dancers. I ran for and was elected to the board of the musicians' union, mainly to get them to change the sexist language that referred to musicians as men. After a long struggle, most of that was changed by a resolution that I drafted.

Through the years, it seems as though people have finally gotten used to seeing an occasional woman in the band—most of the time. And, oh yes! We never had to worry about pay inequity. Scale was the same for men and women . . . always too low.

Karen
Briggs

A violinist who has developed a deep sense of many styles, Manhattan-born Karen Briggs came to international prominence as a featured soloist with Yanni. Since then she has been involved in recording projects with such greats as Stanley Clark and Lenny White. She continues writing and producing her next solo album.

BM: What made you choose the violin?

KB: I started playing violin in junior high school. My father is a saxophonist who came up in the bebop era. His father was a preacher who had his own church and played trumpet and keyboards in the church. My background is in gospel, jazz, R&B, and Caribbean/Latin music. I played with the Virginia symphony for about four years. Basically, I tried to fit myself into any musical situation that I could, whether it was classical or pop. By the time I finished high school I pretty much knew what I wanted to do. And that was to perform. After college I went to New York, gained a reputation for playing gospel, moved to L.A., and got involved in Salsa.

BM: How did you decide on a career in pop music with an untraditional instrument?

KB: It was an ongoing thing, but I often felt very alone because there weren't a lot of people that were doing that. I was met with some resistance because people wondered if I was a serious enough violin player. But I believed in it because the improvisational skills that I was developing were something the other symphony players didn't have. I just took a chance and pursued it as a singular occupation.

BM: So here you are, a woman. You're also an instrumentalist. What kind of problems do we have?
KB: It's an attitude I've tended to overlook. I've always felt that my talent spoke louder than the gender. But at the same time I realize that gender can be a distraction for some people. I've

managed to perform in any number of situations, and it seems like my professionalism and my attitude counted just as much as, if not more than, my talent. If there was someone who had problems with my being a female musician, the relationship lasted as long as it did . . . and then, next. Fortunately, most of the people I've worked with have never done anything to prohibit me from following my dream. I felt that my determination, my attitude, and my belief in what I was doing would make those prejudices a very small setback.

BM: You gained international exposure when you toured with Yanni. Did you notice less resistance toward you as a result of this success?

KB: Life changed drastically for me during this time. A PBS presentation of a concert that we did in Greece, at the Acropolis, gave me international exposure. I had about nine solos. I toured with him for about seven years. Validation was always the key word for me, validation for doing something that a whole lot of people were not doing—playing violin out of its traditional context. The sense of validation from that experience did a lot to drive my confidence level up!

BM: What would you tell any young woman who is embarking on a music career as an instrumentalist?

KB: I would say that the tradeoffs, once you line them all up, are about the same as a 9-to-5 job. You've really got to love it. It's a sound wave that goes up and down, up and down. If you love it enough, the gender aspect will have very little bearing on if you pass or fail. It helps to have a hook to what it is that you do. Try to have a professional attitude. Believe in yourself and don't let anything stop you. Believe in yourself and go with the people who believe in you!

Phyliss Battle

Currently with the Fifth Dimension, Phyliss Battle is always busy with her vocal workshop that helps singers sharpen their skills in all areas of vocal performance. She has toured with many of the superstars but continues forward on the path of the solo artist, teacher, and producer.

BM: You've been on the road with the Fifth Dimension for a long time. What is it about the road that affects you the most?

PB: One thing that affects me a great deal is men's perception about a woman alone on the road. I was in Vegas with Frank and Nancy Sinatra. The show was over, so I went down to the lounge to get a drink and wind down. It was so interesting that the only thing the men thought I was was someone to be picked up . . . as opposed to someone there to enjoy the music. I couldn't sit there and enjoy the music in the lounge because of this perception. This is one of the hazards of being on the road by yourself.

BM: How did you get into the music business?

PB: You know I'm from New York. My cousin took me to the Apollo Theater and got me into the competition, where I ended up in the finals. I got my very first job at a fashion show at a club in Harlem called Small's Paradise. Then this manager got me hooked up on the Canadian hotel circuit doing shows. I dropped out to raise a family. When I got back into it, my first job was with the Donna Summer tour.

BM: From the early days, how have things changed? Have they gotten better?

PB: I think that things have gotten better. However, some of the old problems have just changed form. For instance, a lot of times when the leader is a female, the guys tend to take things for granted. They'll show up late for rehearsal. And then when they get there they're talking about the basketball game last night.

BM: So you feel that the respect level is not there? I'm not sure that it's a *woman* thing, it may be a *musician* thing. I have the same problems with my rehearsals.

PB: And I don't want to get any bad labels, but on the other hand, I'm paying you for this rehearsal and I would expect a certain level of respect. Well . . . not necessarily so. And then we get somewhere, and it's clear that I'm the one in charge, often the venue will bypass me and go directly to one of the guys to find out what's up. It's not that I get bent out of shape about that, but it's one of those things that make you go . . . *Hmmm*!

BM: What would you tell a young woman who's about to go on the road?

PB: Know your craft backwards and forwards. If you have your act together, they are going to take notice. But if you're up there faking, you can forget it. You'll get no respect whatsoever.

When I first went on the road I was a mule. I took everything in my closet. Forget it! Get a couple of pants and jeans, change the tops. Pay attention to all those little travel tips that make life easier.

With all the time you have, this is the time to learn, practice, and plan what you are going to do with your life.

Chapter 5

....

Thinking 24–7

I often refer to something I heard Bill Cosby say
long ago: "I think 24 hours a day." When I heard that, I realized that's the only way to avoid many of the problems that weigh us down daily. It's not always the intensity of the music business that creates the pressures that lead to burnout. Often it's problems we create ourselves by not taking care of business, leaving things to chance, not communicating, not allowing enough time, and not using common sense. Giggers moan and groan about how tough or unfair things are in the music business, but usually the complainer hasn't done jack-squat to further his or her career. Too many of us think that the world of music is a magic carpet ride, from the garage to superstardom. It ain't. It's blood, sweat, and tears—and then you still might not get the gig.

Many of us think that we have to push ourselves to the limit in order to achieve our goals. I'm not talking about your classic hard-working gigger. I'm talking about the manic Type-A personality who will try to squeeze three gigs into one day, work 20 hours straight in a recording studio without a break, and go for days without eating a righteous meal. This kind of activity is necessary for less-than-secure types, just to assure them that they are alive and doing something. They seem to be in a race to a pot of gold that will disappear if they don't reach it yesterday. But the irony of the whole "rush, rush, capture the music business now" scenario is that most of that frantic effort is counterproductive and usually harmful to your health.

If there is any business that can be harmful to your health, it's the one we're in. Late hours, poor diet, smoke-filled clubs, lugging equipment, job insecurity, an uncertain future—all these factors can create the pressures that lead to burnout, of which there are two distinct types. The first kind of burnout I call the "physical-professional," which is common among musicians. The second I call the "spiritual-emotional," which can be much more serious. I'll deal with the "physical-professional" burnout using examples that you'll all experience at some point.

As musicians, we have to take gigs as they come—"making hay while the sun shines," as they say. But when you're offered two gigs in one day, although it means more of the sought-after bread, you should ask yourself if you can give 100% to both jobs. On the first gig, you may lay back because you know you have another job to go to. And on the second gig, you may arrive rushed, funky, and hungry because you got caught in traffic and haven't had time to eat. When you begin to look at gigs for their dollar value only, you begin to diminish the spiritual value of the craft. In other words, the primary purpose of music should not be to see how many notes you can squeeze into a day or how much money you can squeeze out of each gig. The primary purpose should be to give 100% of your creative juices for the uplifting and joy of your environment. If you arrive with that most unselfish purpose, you're gonna get paid!

How about when you work in the studio nonstop, without break or pause? You will have to deal with the issue of diminishing returns. The longer you stay in the studio, the less you're going to get. After three or four hours of intense concentration, being bombarded with the widest range of frequencies, it's time to go home. You are not hearing what you heard when you began, and as you continue you will not hear in the morning what you're hearing now. It's much like effective studying: You'll learn more studying for short periods and taking breaks than trying to ingest an entire book in one sitting.

Nutrition, which is a whole other subject, is as important to your performance as your charts. You cannot give 100% if you have no calories left to burn. Sometime you may try to perform off of caffeine, nicotine, or other substances that give a temporary lift but fail to supply nutrients to rejuvenate the body and brain. The problem is that you're not thinking ahead to give yourself time to sit and eat. You eat on the run or not at all, or you try to eat on the band break, chewing very little. That doesn't work.

Thinking 24 hours a day—that's the bomb. When you go to bed, make a mental plan of what to do in the morning. As you sleep, dream melodies and changes. When you get up, make a mental outline of your day. Think about your gig that night, what you'll need, and how to get there (early). With consistent thought and regular planning, you remove yourself from the edge. Time slows down, pressure diminishes, and burnout is avoided.

There is a more serious burnout that I'll discuss later, but first I must go to the mountaintop to find further enlightenment.

Gregg Field

Gregg Field is a thinking man. He began at a high level at a young age when he became the drummer for the Count Basie Orchestra. It was a dream he had had as a child that became a reality. From there he continued to grow, working with many music greats, most notably Frank Sinatra. As the drummer on Sinatra's *Duets* album, it could be said that he has recorded with more name artists than any contemporary drummer. When not on the road, Field spends much of his time producing projects for artists in the high-tech studio he built in his home.

BM: I don't know many musicians who have spent any more time on the road than you have.

GF: In the fourth grade I had been playing trumpet, until I got my front teeth knocked out in an accident. My father had rented me a set of drums to play with this garage rock band, so when I had the accident I decided to keep on playing drums. And I never looked back.

BM: So you studied formally?

GF: I was lucky, because in my elementary school we had a lot

Gregg Field and vocalist Monica Mancini.

of music courses and a concert band. In my high school we had a concert and jazz band, orchestra, and marching band. But how I got my break is unbelievable. You're not going to believe this, but hopefully it can be an inspiration to someone.

BM: Well go ahead! We'll call this section "Gregg's Story."
GF: My parents took me to Disneyland when I was about 10 years old. I had never heard of Count Basie . . . I had never seen a big band. I was running all around. Then I saw this big crowd gather. The curtains opened up and here's Basie's band, with Sonny Payne playing drums. I had been playing drums for about a year and I was shocked. I couldn't believe it. When we went home I asked my father to buy every Count Basie album he could find. Every day I would come home and study all of the drum parts. I knew the ride cymbal patterns, I knew

when he played the bass drum, the hi-hat. And then I started dreaming about playing with the Count Basie Band. I continued playing the music in my high school band.

And then my mother used to say, "If you really want to be in that band you've got to dream about it. You've got to close your eyes and see yourself there." I thought she was crazy, but I wanted it so bad I was going to try anything. So when I would finish practicing I'd close my eyes and see myself playing with the band.

When I was a senior in high school the Basie Band came to San Francisco. I was taken backstage to meet him. The whole band gets on stage and Basie is waiting in the wings to be introduced. This guy walks up to us and says, "Hey Base, Sonny Payne's not here." Basie turned to me and said, "Didn't you say you were a drummer?" I said, "Yes." He said, "Do you want to play?" And I said, "Yeah." And I marched myself out onstage.

BM: Wow! Is that fate or what?

GF: It's fate. And I played every tune that I had played in my mind or on record hundreds of times. Now, everybody in my high school band knew how obsessed I was about playing in the Basie Band, and this was on a Saturday night. The reason it happened was that they had been doing concerts all week with Ella Fitzgerald, at eight o'clock. Saturday they did an early show and Sonny Payne forgot. So that Monday I went back to school and was telling the guys that I had played with Basie, and they all said, "You are full of it! But what had happened . . . a photographer at the theatre heard that this kid was playing with Basie, and he took all kinds of pictures. And I have those photographs. The other weird thing was that the whole band showed up wearing grey suits. That was exactly what I had on.

So when I walked out on stage I even looked like I was part of the band.

BM: You eventually worked with the Basie band, didn't you?

GF: Sonny Payne left shortly after that, and Butch Miles joined the band. It's good I didn't get called then because I didn't have the chops. My first break out of high school was the Tommy Dorsey Band. Then I went with Ray Charles for about a year, Harry James for about a year and a half. And from there I got drafted into the Basie Band. I spent three years with Count Basie and recorded four albums with him. Man, it was my ultimate dream.

I am convinced that I had put so much energy into wanting to do it that it wasn't about coincidence. When I talk to players, particularly in schools, and ask them who they dream about playing with, some will have the answer right there. Others will say, "I don't know." But I am convinced that if you have a strong passion about wanting to do something, that in itself will create the opportunity. Of course, you have to do the work. I feel blessed that I'm doing what I'm doing in this highly competitive business, but I'm convinced that it's because I just wanted it so much. If you want it enough it'll happen. The universe works in mysterious ways.

PART 1
....
CONCLUSION

The music business is a living thing, a beautiful
yet vicious animal that sometimes eats its young. It is important that you know what it is . . . and who you are. If you are
able to do an honest self-evaluation, analyzing your strengths
and weaknesses early on, you will be way ahead of the game. A
person who has a fear of animals wouldn't rush into veterinary
school. A person with an aversion to blood would probably
not enjoy life as a paramedic. Someone who is vertically chal-
lenged wouldn't normally make a spot on the L.A. Lakers basketball team a primary goal in life. In music there are traits
that, though they don't guarantee success, would probably
make life in the business and on the road a bit more palatable.

How do you handle *fear*? I'm not talking about the fear
of being alone in the dark or anything like that. I mean the
fear of success, the fear of failure, the fear of rejection, the
fear of confrontation, the fear of competition, and so on.
All of those issues that are an integral part of life are somehow magnified in the life of a musician. The musician has to
develop an understanding of fear and how to deal with it in
order to avoid becoming food for the *business*.

A good way to deal with fear is to: (1) study your craft,
(2) practice 'till your hands are about to drop off, and (3)
discuss and read about every aspect of the business. It's the

difference between walking into a test knowing the answers and going in unprepared. You know the feeling.

How do you feel about *people*? Art is about people. Art is about one person expressing an idea to another person in order to solicit some type of response. We use music, but it is definitely a *people thing*. If you don't have a really positive attitude toward people, it will be reflected in your music. (If you are a negative person and you dig the dark side of things, this book is not for you.) But if you want to move, along with your music, to a higher level, we can talk. Being sensitive and caring about people is the first step to being a *real* musician, not necessarily a rich or famous one, but a *real* one.

Figure out a way to become comfortable around people. Even if you're a dork. Begin to initiate conversations with your family and friends. Then try sharing some amenities like "How are you today?" with total strangers. You may find out that interacting with people is no big deal. It's just something you may have to practice a little.

As a musician, it's a must that you learn how to make commonsense decisions, that you learn how to *think* (not to be confused with dreaming). It is extremely easy to lose perspective in a world without form, without apparent rules. But there are rules. The same rules everyone else has to follow. They just get bent from time to time in the music business and in other industries that don't follow federal guidelines.

To begin to get a handle on some of the rules, you must: (1) know that you don't make any of them, (2) realize that the rules that do exist are here for a reason, (3) understand that when you make up your own rules you do so at your own risk. Talk to people who are successful to see how they've gone about their business. Talk to the guy on the corner who's bumming a quarter to learn what *not* to do.

PART 2

·····················

YOUR BAND

Relating to Other Musicians

Regardless of your performance situation—solo, duo, trio, big band, or whatever—one of the most challenging parts of gigging is dealing with other musicians. While you can learn something about how to do this from the bevy of business management books available, they will not give you all the tools you need, because you are dealing with musicians, not MBAs. Learn how to motivate and work with other giggers, and the gig becomes a magical and inspiring place. Fail at this task, and watch your promising act or project fall victim to personality conflicts and conflicting agendas.

This is not to say that honing your people skills will result in conflict-free relationships. Indeed, some of the best and most popular music ever made was created by folks who all but hated one another. (The guys who make up The Who are classic examples. Their fights are legendary, and so is some of the music they produced.) Just like great music, great relationships in the music business are all about tension and release, conflict and resolution. The goal is to get there without bloodshed.

Chapter 6

....

Split Personalities, or the Eight Faces of a Bandleader

Although many factors contribute to the breakup of groups, none is as important as leadership. With bands, leadership is often assumed rather than earned. It is usually assumed by the person who brings the group together or gets the gig. It doesn't always have to do with ability.

One of the many great myths we live with is that of the "born leader." No one is born a leader per se. No one climbs out of the womb telling the doctor what to do. I don't think there are "born athletes" or "born musicians." Of course there are those with a stronger disposition and certain psychophysiological traits that enable them to excel in certain areas, but your experience and environment shape all of this and set the direction to go into sports, music, arts, politics, or whatever. No matter what gifts you're born with, you have to work your butt off to develop them.

The following is my list of leader types you may come across as a gigger. These involve traits that you may have inherited yourself without realizing it. And these traits can drive you nuts.

- The Hitlerian is the total control freak, able to sway the band through the power of personality and able to agree only when everything is done his/her way, even when it ain't working. The Hitlerian band leader is usually driven by a deeply rooted inferiority complex.

- The Machiavellian functions by doing or saying anything it takes to get the band or the gig. Such a leader has few spiritual ties to the band. No player is indispensable if it means a better situation for him/her. This kind of person is success oriented but usually lacks compassion.

- The Pope Pius wants the nightclub experience to be spiritual. This is good up to a point. But in reality, the nightclub experience is rough and earthy. The Pope Pius leader doesn't want to get dirty. There are no confrontations, no fighting. And although quite ethical, he/she seldom takes responsibility for any bad decision. Everything is beautiful.

- The Illusionist gives the appearance of being in control, but it is only an illusion. This kind of leader plays off the ideas and creativity of the group before initiating any action. This is the type you give an idea to on Friday, and Monday they give it back to you like it was their idea. This leader is short on foresight and will do a disappearing act during conflict.

- The Harrisimo (Hare) is a firecracker who sets up the band in a flood of inspired ideas that quickly dissipate to nothing. The Harrisimo lacks the ability to follow through, has little staying power, and will quit if things seem to be at a standstill. This kind of person lacks patience and wants to complete things in hours that should take days (like putting a good show together).

- The Tortissimo (Tortoise) leads at his/her own pace which is usually out of sync with reality. The Tortissimo may return a call days later, if at all, and waits until the last minute to do just about everything. This deliberate soul sees no urgency in anything and never any reason to rush, even when late for the gig. What is most frustrating about this type is his/her ability to take days doing what should take only hours.

- The Joy Stick leader approaches everything in terms of fun—not business. As long as everyone is having fun, it's OK, whether it makes money or not. This type of person simply does not feel up to dealing with the stark realities of life and has not learned that it is OK to get pissed off.

- The Reaper (Grim) looks at the business and everyone in it in a negative light. "All agents and club owners are scumbags and jerks," is the mantra of the Reaper. The only reason he/she is in the business, a reaper will condescendingly explain, is because it is the lesser of two evils.

There are probably many more types of leaders, but these are the ones I know. I myself have been them, and I've made all the mistakes associated with them. It takes a long time to develop leader chops. You have to be able to accept the separation between you and your friends that is created by the leader–sideman relationship. You have to be able to accept the heat, the criticism, and the stress, but most of all you have to be willing to take on the responsibility.

It's important to realize that all these leader types have qualities that are pertinent to success. If you combine the dynamic drive of the Hitlerian with the craftiness of the Machiavellian, the ethics of the Pope Pius, the persona of the

Illusionist, the energy of the Harrisimo, the reserve of the Tortissimo, the positive energy of the Joy Stick, and the Reaper's more accurate perception of the music business, you will have a chance to become a successful leader. It's like playing the blues, rock, swing, and zydeco at the same time. You may not be able to do it physically, but you can stay aware of it all in your mind. Take the attributes, mix them with common sense, then call me so I can play in your band.

Erik
Ekstrand

Eric Ekstrand has toured internationally and has
become a club mainstay on the West Coast. His swing band
appears regularly at Hollywood's famous Derby (as seen in the
film *Swingers*) as well as the Jazz Bakery and the new Coconut
Club. He has been typecast as Hollywood's piano player and
can be seen as Frank Sinatra's accompanist in HBO's *The Rat
Pack* and *Introducing Dorothy Dandridge*.

BM: Eric, your band is slammin. You have a very upbeat style
that creates a happy atmosphere for the band and the audience. How did you create that style?

EE: My dad was a very good musician who had played with Benny Goodman, Shep Fields, Paul Whiteman, and he was on staff at CBS. I grew up meeting people like Teddy Wilson, Urbie Green, Hank Jones, because these were my father's contemporaries and friends. So I was greatly influenced by that. I started playing professionally when I was about 14. I started with clarinet and switched to piano when I was about 11. As a teen I played with various rock bands. And then we moved to Vegas and I played some of the show rooms and at the same time became involved with recording, on the engineering side. Came to L.A. in '75 and worked as a sideman until I started my own band in the '80s. About 1990 I decided to put together my swing band. I began writing the book, began rehearsing the band in '92, and we've been working ever since.

BM: I thought this was something you had been doing all along.

EE: No, I've been doing all kinds of stuff. I've always been influenced by swing and jazz because that's what was played around the house—Count Basie, Woody Herman, big band music.

BM: As a bandleader, how were you influenced by your experiences as a sideman?

EE: A lot! I think I learned as much what *not* to do as what to do. One of the reasons I've been able to keep a band of some of L.A.'s finest musicians together for so long is that I try not to make those kind of mistakes. When I was a sideman I sometimes felt as though I was being mistreated, that my contributions to the music were being ignored. You have to really appreciate what everyone is contributing. It's not enough to just say it. You have to mean it. Because you wouldn't have a band if not for these other players working with you.

Being a bandleader is like any other position of leadership. One thing I've always held in my heart is that if you want to lead, first you have to serve. You have to give your musicians something that will make them want to continue doing it. In my case I try to pay as well as I can, and even when the gigs don't pay that well the guys still come out. I try to give them respect as musicians and music that they'll enjoy playing.

The whole impetus to this band that I'm doing is *fun*. Everything has to be fun for me, for the musicians, and mostly for the audience.

BM: What are some other things you learned as a sideman?
EE: Some of those positive things. Everyone wants to feel important . . . it's human nature. As a bandleader it's your job to make everybody in the band feel like an integral part of the operation, which, of course, they are.

BM: What do you say to a musician who is about to form a band, perhaps for the first time?
EE: For one, you have to really be careful who you choose. The hardest thing for me was having to let guys go. It's a heartbreaker. And sometimes it takes days or weeks to build up the courage. The musicians end up being your friends. I've had to let some good friends go because musically it wasn't happening anymore. So try to be real clear about what you want from your band

Second, you really have to respect the guys who are coming to work with you. They're coming and rehearsing for nothing, and you have to appreciate that contribution that they're making. You wouldn't have a band without them.

You wouldn't have a show without an audience, so really appreciate your audience too. That's what it's all about. That's how you reach people. Otherwise, you might as well stay at home and play for yourself. If you're going to start a band you are going to have to interact with people, and that's the hardest thing of all. That's even harder than learning how to play your instrument.

Chuck
Wansley

Chuck Wansley is a dynamic performer and the
consummate bandleader. Born in New York, he was a Motown
Records and Prism recording artist, formerly with the group
WARP 9. Chuck is Los Angeles' hottest party and concert band,
playing music from the 1940s, '50s, swing, pop, R&B, jazz,
disco, as well as the current styles.

BM: Take us back to the beginning.
CW: I attribute a lot of my music to my father, who took me
to music events and concerts when I was a tot. I was too young

for clubs. But he'd take me to see James Moody, Dizzy Gillespie, Thad Jones, and everybody. So, I got introduced at a young age. In fourth grade they had this deal where kids could take up instruments. I rented some sticks and a pad and decided to become a drummer. At the time I didn't know that my father had been a drummer. He had never told me. I just gravitated to it. They laughed when they told me the story. My dad was a drummer until he began raising a family, and then the drums became the coffee table. My family never encouraged me to become a musician. However, there was music around our home constantly. They were surprised when I stuck with it on my own.

BM: When did you start singing?

CW: I sang in the church choir. It wasn't a "down–home" gospel church. My grandmother's was a down-home church. When we moved out to Long Island, the neighborhood was a little different and I ended up singing in an Episcopal church. I started young, but I trained my voice that way. In tenth grade I was playing drums in my cousin's band, and the singer came late and I started filling in on backups. Of course, later on in life I jumped off of the drums because I was tired of playing for nonsingers.

BM: You said, "I can do this," huh?

CW: Yeah! Drummers are always the first one to the gig and the last one to leave. I decided that I was going to be a singer instead. And now I'm a bandleader. I'm still the first one to the gig and the last one to leave . . . because there are so many responsibilities. I was playing with a band at a very young age. And although my father didn't really try to discourage me, he was hoping that the club experience would deter me. It didn't.

BM: I'd like you to share some of the things that it took time for you to learn. You have such a great band, and you seem to have an equally great rapport with your musicians.

CW: That old expression "Check your egos at the door"? You hear musicians bragging about how good they are and where they've been. It's all about the moment and what you're creating at that time. And you need to come in open and free. No matter what genre you're in or what level you're at, you have to come to give and at the same time keeping your eyes and ears open. Because everyone has something to offer. Even the poorest of musicians have something to offer. They might have something that you can spark off of if you just keep your ears open. You've got to stay there and not play for yourself. If you feed off of each other, you are really going to create.

BM: What problems did you face as you were putting your bands together?

CW: Well, it's kind of difficult to explain. I'd have to begin with the pressures of sometimes having to be like a coach, sometimes a counselor. You have to keep everybody happy, yet in the same stroke be a leader. It's a little different for me because I never saw myself as a real leader. Although I like being there in the front, I think of myself as one of the "cats." I come from the bottom parts so I know what it's like to be a sideman. So I treat my guys like everyone's the same. And I don't try to be a Hitler, on top of everybody, talking about you have to do this or do that. By me paying attention to so many styles of music, I think they're a little surprised when ideas I come up with are old style and new style. So there's a respect there, as long as I treat everyone the same.

BM: Do musicians ever take you for granted and step past your leadership? And if so, how do you deal with it?

CW: Occasionally! Yes, I've gotten into a few scuffles. I try to sit back and think of it as the moment. Kind of like maybe someone had a really bad day. Why should I get into a fighting, screaming argument? Although I have at times. I come back to them later. I step back and keep the steam in instead of letting it all out, and try to see it from their viewpoint. If someone just can't gel, then maybe they shouldn't be in the band. But I've never had that problem. I try to look for the best part in people . . . and draw that out. *Care* is the word. If someone feels as though they're cared about, they want to give their best all the time, no matter who they are.

BM: Where do you find such versatile musicians?
CW: I don't actually go out and look, although I try different people. It's like fate brings them and they end up staying, whoever the right people are. I have a certain standard and the word gets around. So a sub knows that he's going to have to be versed. The job does require some reading at times. And that's just something that all musicians have to stay boned up on . . . including myself. I have a reputation for wanting to experience the whole spectrum of music, and it encourages the band members to check out the different styles.

BM: I wish I had met you many years ago.

Chapter 7

. . . .

The Big "Mo"

Momentum. It's the idea of movement and the force
behind it, the energy that keeps things happening. Momentum
keeps sharks from sinking, pushes homes and trees down hill-
sides, and carries athletes and politicians to victory. And if you
don't have enough, it can lead to the breakup of relationships—especially bands.

I've discussed some of the issues that can disrupt the
progress of groups, such as poor leadership and unclear roles.
But the lack of momentum, movement, or progress can eat
away at the enthusiasm and take the heart out of the music
and the band. There are many signs that will indicate that your
band and your music may be bogged down and not moving. If
your band is playing the same tunes and the same gigs and
arguing about the same things, there may be a lack of momentum. If you go to your gig and you know everyone in the audi
ence by first name, it may be a lack of the big "mo." (Whether
you have platinum on the wall or you've been playing the same
stuff.) When band members start sending subs to rehearsal,
are you missing the big "mo"? When it's time to hit and you

don't even feel like tuning up, you'd better check out the big "mo."

Momentum can be affected by the band itself. Too often band members want to leave the "dirty" work (business) up to "the other guy" or the leader. Musicians dodge work and responsibility with statements like "I just want to play my instrument, man," or "I didn't join the band to do paperwork." But the reality is that the whole band has to initiate, develop, and maintain the momentum that will carry them to success. The driving force cannot be the sole responsibility of a leader, a record label, or a manager. If it's a group, then it has to be a group effort. A great gigger treats every musical situation like it is his/her very own. If you hold back because it's not "your" band, then you are shortchanging yourself, the music, and the musicians with whom you share the stage.

One or two people can't do everything that needs to be done to create a successful working situation: booking, rehearsing, negotiating, planning, promoting, and publicizing, or just letting all your friends know where the next perform-ance is. Playing music is the major function, but not the only function, of a band. The momentum is creating the band itself.

The individual affects momentum by his/her attitude toward the band and the concept of self. There is a positive attitude that musicians and bands must have that declares, "Hey, my music is good! It's important and it needs to be shared with others." This upbeat attitude will keep the old "mo" working. A band's momentum is fed by each musician's positive input and enthusiasm. The music business is full of scenarios that lead to burnout, disappointment, or self-doubt. All are forms of negativity that will distract you from your goals. Don't go for it! When a musician loses confidence and enthusiasm, he or she is on the way to losing the dream.

Becoming complacent on one particular gig can affect momentum. Although regular gigs can be lucrative and secure to a point, they can also lure you into believing that this is what music is about. And it ain't! I've seen musicians grow old on gigs, having done nothing else to contribute to the world of music or develop self but make that gig night after night, year after year. It may pay bills, but it will leave you with nothing for musical or personal development. It will leave you nothing but a gold watch at retirement. This may be enough for some (duh!), but music itself is about creativity, adventure, change, growth—and momentum. There are so many experiences waiting for even the most complacent band: street and food festivals, local cable shows, parks and recreational events, senior citizens' programs, school concerts. In short, there are all kinds of events that give you the opportunity to play, increase your following, and make a few bucks. By keeping your band busy doing different things, you'll be able to respond to the classic question "What have you done lately?"

Momentum is not just a force; it's a force that grows stronger and stronger. I think that its most important ingredient is faith. If a band has faith in their music and faith in their ability to perform it, it's even easier to continue on that faith together, even when there are few gigs in sight. If you have faith in the future, then when everyone else sees nothing, you'll be able to see that glint of platinum at the end of the tunnel. I developed a faith, in the biblical sense, that's helped me to hang on even when times were hard. Once you establish the big "mo" as a band or musician, then do all you can to keep from losing it. Do all you can to make it stronger so that it'll carry you where you have to go.

Larry
Hathaway

Larry Hathaway is a lifelong music enthusiast, with extensive experience in sales, marketing, and production. He has had tenure with such labels as Concord, JVC, and Capitol and produced several projects featuring such artists as Poncho Sanchez, Mel Torme, Earnie Watts, and Rosemary Clooney, to name a few.

BM: Did you begin your career in the business as a musician?
LH: Actually, my father was a musician during the big band era and also owned a record store. I worked there as a child and later began working for a record store chain. From that chain I was hired by Capitol Records in sales and marketing. Later I went to work for Blue Note as sales manager.

BM: As a promotion person you do one thing. What are some of the things that bands should do that they often don't do?
LH: At some point bands have to think more like businesspeople than like musicians. The way to do that is to get out and meet record people, music and club people, people who are in the business, and try to get some real "street knowledge" that way. There are too many people that go into the music business thinking that just because they have talent they will have success. And most of them aren't [successful]. Most of the

ones that are successful have natural business tendencies that they can use. Unless you have a fluke, the most successful artists are the ones who worked hard in the business, going out to the radio stations, record stores, interviews, and really *working* every record. Not just the first record, but every record that they came out with.

I think it's a common fallacy for young bands and young people in general. They think they know how it all works because they took a few business courses in school. But in reality they really don't know what the *street* is all about, what the *real* music scene is all about. The most important thing that a young band can do is to get out and meet the people.

BM: I notice a lot of musicians stay isolated in their own little world. And when they leave the studio, they are lost.

LH: Musicians have to be able to understand what it takes to make someone take notice. You have to be able to promote yourself before you can promote your music. You can be a great piano player, but if you're shy and into yourself, not willing to go out and interact with people, that's all you're going to be . . . a good piano player. You aren't going to be a recording star, a personality that someone can sell, or anything like that. If you are shy, you have to force yourself out of that shell so that you can promote yourself and make people take notice of you and your music.

I remember, years ago my secretary came into my office and said, "We're being picketed." So we went out in front of the Capitol tower, on Vine, and here was a rock band walking up and down the street with picket signs. The signs read, "CAPITOL WON'T LISTEN TO OUR DEMO." It was probably true, seeing that the A&R guys were buried in product. But what it did was bring attention to this band, who was saying, "Hey, look . . . do something for us!" And they did listen to them. I don't think they were signed, but they were heard. There have been all kinds of gimmicks that bands have used to get themselves heard, but it all boils down to *self-promotion*.

Chapter 8

· ·

Understand, Understanding. . . Understood?

One event that occurs too often in the music world is the breakup of bands bands with great potential, whose lives are cut short before they even get started. Too often bands break up for all the stupid reasons. When I say *stupid*, I mean problems that could have been avoided in the beginning, with a little conversation. The old-timers used to say, "A good understanding is the best thing in the world." There are several things in life that I've enjoyed more than a good understanding, but I do understand the relevance of the statement.

In the entertainment business, breaking up is a natural phenomenon—necessary, painful, and discouraging. Breaking up feeds the emotional pool of the musician. The developing musician and band have to go through the same changes as a tune. We musicians must grow, develop, expand, and experience as much as we can while we can. We should seek new scenes, new music, new concepts. But sometimes, these breakups can have a negative effect. They can alter our perception of the music business and of life, and may rob us of the desire to continue. These types of life experiences act as a filter that strains out those of us who haven't committed to a life of gigging. But it can also destroy potential talent before it begins to develop.

I've seen a lot of bands go through a lot of changes. I've seen bands break up, and it made me feel bad. Several things have led to the breakup of bands I was in or leading. Three of those were (1) poorly defined roles, (2) poor leadership and organization, and (3) the lack of momentum and progress. Of course, musicians move in and out of groups when there is an opportunity to make more bread or when they just get tired of putting up with the same old B.S.

When the band first comes together, you jam, rehearse, check one another out, and see who does what. The next and most logical step should be sitting down to talk about issues, desires, and possibilities. This rarely happens. Musicians are into the music and want to leave legal issues to lawyers. We tend to expect things to work themselves out. But they don't. It is important that band members sit down together and deal with questions concerning their future—to lay the groundwork, the mechanics of the group—in the beginning. Here are some of the questions your band should chew on:

- Who is the leader?
- If there is no leader, how does the group make music and business decisions?
- How do we choose the tunes?
- If we write together, is it 50–50 or what?
- Who hustles the gigs?
- Who talks to the clubs, agents, and managers?

These questions should be raised before the money starts coming in, because we all know that money has a tendency to change people.

Something as simple as writing a tune with someone can lead to multimillion-dollar legal nightmares, if the proper understanding isn't reached up front. No one is concerned about the legal side of publishing when they're back in the garage struggling to create a tune. This issue has destroyed bands and friendships, and wasted millions of dollars in court costs. And all of that could have been avoided with a little "understanding." It is important to form that understanding from the beginning, because things have a way of changing, especially when the specter of success rears its corrupting and enticing head. Musicians will lay back to see what's going to happen and let whomever exercises the initiative expend the energy. But when it comes time to cut the pie, everyone wants an equal slice. This can be a problem—especially for the one who's been busting his or her behind.

So if you decide to choose a leader for your group, choose the one who is articulate, has some business sense, and doesn't mind getting up in the morning and squaring off with the world. Don't pick someone to lead your group because they're the best player, the most charismatic onstage, or have the best equipment. These things have very little to do with negotiating contracts. Select the one who expresses the desire to lead and has the energy and mindset to do so. If you choose to make decisions by committee, prepare to take a little longer to get from point A to point B. And remember, it's important to figure out a way to eliminate all ego from your group decision-making process.

Another route would be to include one of your friends who expresses an interest in the entertainment business but who is not necessarily a musician. If you could get one of your friends interested in management, you could end up with a manager who knows and cares about the group and grows along with the band in knowledge and experience. Remember, if everyone wants equal money, everyone should do equal work.

If you are putting a band together, I hope this chapter is helpful. Just remember what the old-timers used to say: "Understanding is the best thing in the world."

Poncho Sanchez

Perhaps no other group on the music scene today exhibits more sense of family and togetherness than the band led by Poncho Sanchez. For almost two decades they have worked toward being one of the world's most celebrated Latin jazz bands. And now they have arrived. Poncho Sanchez has been an unswervingly passionate exponent of the bedrock style of Afro-Cuban jazz pioneered half a century ago by such legends as Machito, Tito Puente, and Dizzy Gillespie. Raised in

Southern California, he and his band are the undisputed leaders of a vibrant hybrid that's become one of the most dynamic and enduring popular styles. This music speaks with equal passion to dancers and listeners as well. It is the very definition of Grammy-winning Latin soul.

BM: Whenever I discuss your group, I mention the strong, family-like ties within the band that I believe contribute to your tremendous success and consistency. Although you guys aren't related, you are like family.

PONCHO: That is absolutely true. The Poncho Sanchez Latin Jazz Band is run like a family . . . especially in the beginning, to unite and stay together. You know what I mean?

'Cause in the early years we weren't making any money at all, just playing and makin' a little bit of bread for our gas money. But for me it all started back with my family. I'm the youngest of 11 kids. I've got six sisters and four brothers. My mother and father lived a very good life. They both died at 88 and 87 years old. So they lived a long life and a beautiful life. And so it starts a lot in the home, I think. With my mother and father, they had very fine qualities and they wanted us to continue that and carry on that tradition. And so I feel that I have made them proud because they instilled that in us when we were kids . . . that you've got to study, work hard, be honest, and things will happen for you. You know what I mean? And believe in the Lord and all like that. So I come from that. Being the youngest I got away with a lot of stuff, but I also had my brothers and sisters to look up to. I learned a great deal by watching them. When you come up with something like that, it's going to stay with you.

BM: What were the early days like for you?

PONCHO: I wasn't that great of a student, but most of my brothers and sisters were. In those days there were no schools to learn this kind of music. Nowadays kids have all sorts of ways to learn, and I say they should take advantage of it. Because we didn't have that when we were growing up. Now they have videotapes—how to play Latin music, how to play mambo, cha-cha-cha, congas, timbales—they actually have videos of that today. They have play-along CDs. We didn't have any of that.

BM: At the college I went to you were not allowed to play jazz in the music building.

PONCHO: See what I'm saying? Today there is a big difference, and I'm glad it turned out the way it is. I say take advantage of it! You can go to a music store and take conga and timbale lessons. When I was growing up you ask a guy to give you a conga lesson and he'd probably laugh at you: "What are you talking about, man?" They would give you a drum lesson or sax or trumpet lesson, but not a conga drum lesson.

BM: One of the hardest things in the music business is keeping a band together. You are one of the few groups that I know of that has been able to stay together . . . aside from the regular changes. How does that happen?

PONCHO: We'll soon be celebrating the release of our 20th anniversary CD and also 20 years as a band. Actually, the band started with Ramon Banda and Tony Banda, timbales and bass, Ramon played trap drums, Sal Cracchiolo played trumpet, Dick Mitchell played saxophone, and Charlie Ottwell played piano. And they had already put the band together and were doing jazz and Latin jazz tunes. I was on the road with Cal Tjader, and whenever I'd come into town . . . Those are my brothers, you know what I mean? They would invite me to rehearse with them. So I'd bring some charts that I had picked up on the road, and we'd play them a little bit.

We did that for about six months, and then we said, "Hey, the band needs a name!" So we called the band Montuno and we got a few small gigs. Everybody started calling me on the gig because I was the guy on the mic, I sang a couple of tunes and announced. But it was *our* band, and everybody thought it was my band. So little by little I started booking more gigs, bringing more charts, and calling the shots a little more. So about a year and a half goes by. I was doing a lot of work with that part of it. So I said, "You know what? Why don't we just call it the Poncho Sanchez Latin Jazz Band?" Everybody said, "That's cool with us . . . no problem." So I made some cards up, you know, the whole thing.

BM: Did you continue taking care of the business?
PONCHO: Actually, Ruth Roby, who had been with the Monterey Jazz Festival, started managing us first and booking us on some local gigs. So when we started out they were small gigs. But we loved the music and loved the band. The Banda brothers and Sal Cracchiolo, whom I met when I was in the jazz band at Cerritos College, are still in the band today. It's the family thing that has kept it together. Because we're more like family, you know. We said, "We'll just do some gigs, and we'll hang together." We enjoyed each other and we all loved the music. And so it was important for us to keep the band together. And that's how it starts.

BM: I contend that in order to have a successful band everyone should be responsible for doing something to promote the band. Do you find that to be true?
PONCHO: In the early years, yes. It was a little easier because all of us were really into it. Everybody made little cards up and

would pass them out to all their friends and try to find any kind of little gig that you can. And it can start out good like that. But to be honest with you, the only way that's going to work is if you're young, in high school or college, and you are trying to put a band together. But once you get past that . . . Like today, there's a lot of professional musicians. If you try to pull them together to do something . . . well, they're all thinking, "Hey, I've got my own thing happening, my own CD, my own future." That's why that's hard, when you deal with musicians that have passed that limit.

BM: What about within the band, within the family? Does everyone have some kind of role to take care of certain things?
PONCHO: No, not anymore! Just in the early years. And you've got to do it that way, because it's impossible for one person to do everything. You've got to have some sort of help. So that's very true . That's the way it should work, and that's the way it worked for me at the beginning. But then I got into the agents, and their people start making the phone calls. And then Ruth said, "Poncho, you need a promotional package." And we started with those baby steps.

BM: What is the bottom line for a successful band?
PONCHO: To become successful . . . or to have a half of a chance . . . the key things, depending on what stage you're at: First of all you have to have a good band. You have to have your own original music, someone in the band writing and arranging or whatever you want to do. You've gotta have your music together. Myself, I don't read or write and I've written about 15 or 20 tunes, but I write them through piano players. They physically write it out as I hum all the parts. You've got to have a music director, which I've always had, to help me with my ideas. Or if you are the leader, make sure that your

book is together, with the parts all straightened out. Then you have to hook up with some type of agency, to help you get some gigs, or a manager and management team. And as your bookings increase, now you have to hook up with a travel agent to help you with tickets, schedules, and all that. Often a venue will provide all the travel arrangements, but sometimes it is included in your fee. So it would be up to your travel agent to get the best deal for the band.

BM: Talking about taking care of business, what was a memorable experience that reflects when business was not being taken care of.

PONCHO: Just off the top of my head, something hilarious that happened just recently. We've played Carnegie Hall twice already. Now, that's a pretty big gig. I mean it doesn't get much bigger than that. I remember when I was a kid they said if you get to Carnegie Hall you've made it. Well, I've been there twice and hopefully there's more coming.

The first time I played was Fathers Day a couple of years ago, and it was really special. Mongo Santamaria is my hero. I even named my son after him and everything like that. I learned a lot by listening to his records and watching him play. And now Mongo Santamaria is one of my best friends. He and his daughter came to see us, and as we were sitting in the dressing room, I flashed: Here the master was sitting watching me tape my hands. And I said: Whoa! I remember when I was a kid, I used to sit and watch him tape his hands. And I looked at him and I asked, "Teacher, would you like to play with me tonight?" We featured him as our special guest on "Afro Blue," which he wrote. And he got a standing ovation before we played and an encore after we played. That was just a very special thing for me and Mongo and all that.

We played Carnegie Hall again last year. And a funny thing that happened this time: We get to New York and everybody's luggage arrived but mine. Well now, at Carnegie Hall you want to wear your very best. The cats had their nice suits on, everybody was looking sharp. I had a sharp suit too, but it was in my luggage. There was no time to buy one. We flew in, sound check, and hit time. When we went out onstage I had to use my experience and wit to explain what had happened. Billy, I had to play Carnegie Hall in street clothes like these. I felt real funny about it, but I said, "I'm going to do it!" Then someone yelled out, "It ain't what you look like, it's the music that we're here for." Then someone yelled, "Hey, Poncho, you look good to me. Just play good!" And I'm glad that we have fans like that. We jumped to it—we hit, and we did great.

PART 2
CONCLUSION

If you have a band, you have a group of individuals coming together with a common purpose. But what if there is no common purpose? You have a bunch of people all doing their own thing, or standing around waiting for something to happen. Without direction or purpose you are not even a group . . . you are a mob, being pulled from one side to the other. Even our lowest life forms have direction and purpose. That's how they have survived for millions of years. Each little cell knows what it has to do to survive. And it does it. If a band lacks this knowledge, its chances of surviving are nil.

As you put your band together, ask yourselves some hard questions:

- Are these the kind of individuals I want to be associated with?
- Do they have the same commitment I have?
- Are there any negative habits that should be dealt with immediately?
- Are our music concepts compatible?

- Do we share the same work ethic?
- Do I like them, and do they like me?

The answers to some of these questions may not be obvious (at first). And you may want to give the circumstance the benefit of the doubt. If you are able to get through that phase, then you are ready to deal with organization. Usually there is a force that sets direction. It may be the power of the music, it may be the strength of a certain personality or the direction set by a production or by management. Whatever the direction, you have to make sure that you are OK with it. The band has to make certain determinations:

- How will we make decisions?
- Who is the leader—he, she, me, or us?
- Am I willing to take direction, or is it necessary that I give direction?
- Do we share responsibilities? And if so, how?
- Do we share deposits, tips, royalties, advances, etc.? And if so, how?
- Who calls the tunes?
- Who does the arrangements?

The list could go on and on.

The most successful bands are those that are consistent, aggressive, and creative. But most importantly, they are the bands that stay together. Bands come and go. Some bands have one or two little hits and then vanish, never to be heard from again. It is the band that has leadership, dedication, and a sense of family that will rise to the top and probably stay there.

PART 3
·····················
YOUR GIG

Taking Care of the Business of Music

Years ago on TV, there was an episode of a sitcom in which a character made reference to someone who had tried to hold up a bank with a staple gun, commenting, "He must have been a musician." Despite the near worship experienced by some musicians, popular culture has most often portrayed us as, let's just say, less than astute in matters of real life and real business. In large part we are to blame. Too many of us have used the old copout of "I'm a creative person, not a businessperson." It's as if we think dealing with business will somehow pollute our muse.

But creativity and business savvy are not mutually exclusive, and these days you treat them as such at your own peril. The truth is that no one cares about your musical career like you do. There is just one person who has your interests at heart at all times and that is you.

Learning how to take care of business will help ensure a lengthy career, and there is no more important element to your success. You cannot count on a manager or record company to take care of your business, no matter how successful you become, so the time to learn is now.

Chapter 9

••••••••••••••••••••••••

What Would "Bird" Say?

I wonder what "Bird" would say if he had to work with musicians who drink vegetable juice and pop vitamins instead of doing drugs? The genius of Charlie Parker was in many ways diminished by the influence his drug use had on other musicians. Although drugs have always been a quietly accepted part of the music culture, one of the greatest lies ever perpetrated is that drugs can enhance performance. Any performer who knows the difference knows the only thing drugs intensify is a false sense of self—not a better performance.

This is a personal issue, one I feel will influence the direction of the next generation of musicians as well as the survival of our present culture. I might be considered liberal when it comes to drugs. How could I, or anyone else, be anything but liberal? We live in a drug culture. The average American starts the day with a cup of coffee (drug), a cigarette (drug), an aspirin (drug) for that throbbing headache, and any number of prescription drugs—all this just to start the day. Although I have voted for legalizing the medical use of marijuana, I would never encourage anyone, especially musicians, to use drugs. I have come to realize that anyone who plans on securing success must eventually learn to deal with the environment naturally, i.e., drug free, spiritually unencumbered. But this chapter is not about the drug scene, but rather about how drugs relate to performance. I'm not concerned with whether one uses drugs, I'm concerned with when one uses drugs.

I'll admit there have been some musical eras that, by their very essence, lent themselves to some type of drug use, whether to expand the musicians' consciousness or to create a "oneness with the universe." Most countercultures have developed their own justifications for using, but recreational drugs create what they are developed to create: a breach with reality. Unless everyone is on the same trip (i.e., every member of the band and every person in the house, in which case nothing matters because no one knows what's going on), there will be a spiritual breach within your being, your band, and your performance. Unfortunately, none of this is evident to you when you are high. This is not unlike the drunk who thinks he is the greatest dancer at the party—until he sees the video the next day.

Put plainly, drugs put you out of step with the One, with yourself, and with your music. They speed you up and slow you down. They erase the edge you need as a musician to apply to your instrument and your performance. If an athlete takes drugs, fans have to wonder if they're getting their money's worth. When public figures do drugs, their validity is put into question. Would you like to see your doctor doing drugs? I think not. So how do we as musicians think we can consume junk and not create some kind of problem? I'm one of those old-fashioned musicians who believes that all music must have spiritual value. If, as an artist, you allow your environment to control you, removing your soul from the natural, you short-change your music, your audience, and the talent God gave you.

I've been a performing and recording artist for many years, many of those under the influence. It worked for a time because my audience didn't know they were only getting 50%. When I committed to taking control of my space and began operating in the natural, things began to change. Fear, which is at the root of most drug use, began to ebb away, and I started to discover new things about myself and my music. People began to enjoy the music—and me—even more as they realized I was giving more of myself. I began to mend the breaches and found I was looking forward to the gig because it was an opportunity to share my real soul.

Drug use is a personal issue. It's a bit much to think that artists are not going to experiment. But I say to any musician who's going to perform for others: Do so with a clear mind and a clear spirit. Once you've given your audience 150% of yourself, what you do after the gig is your business.

Mark
Lennon

Mark Lennon comes from a strong family musical tradition, which began with Bill and Ted Lennon, who sang in a swing group popular in the 1940s and '50s, and Pat Lennon of the Lennon Sisters, from The Lawrence Welk Show. The members of the band Venice grew up in large-family situations and learned how to work together at an early age. The band is like an extension of their family. They are proud traditionalists with rock-solid influences: a beguiling mix of pop, rock, folk, and R&B. Comprising cousins Kipp and Michael Lennon and their respective brothers Pat and Mark Lennon, this suburban Los Angeles quartet steadfastly refuses to succumb to fast-buck trendiness, opting instead for a more humanistic musical approach with their surf-scented harmonies and folk-pop sounds.

BM: Mark, I'm always most curious about how musicians get started.

MARK: The summer of my eighth-grade graduation I was 14. My brother Michael had a band. They were, like, 17. They knew a few cover tunes, and I started singing third-part harmony with them, and it was like, "Wow! This sounds great." We started doing more cover tunes, doing parties—all that.

BM: What did your parents think about your starting so early?

MARK: They loved it. They thought the music was good. It wasn't this hard rock. They loved the harmonies. And here I was making money at 14 years old.

BM: Your family was in the music business?

MARK: My cousins are the Lennon Sisters. Kipp, who's in the band, they're his older sisters. My mom was actually their aunt. I'm the youngest of 13 and Kipp is the youngest of 11.

BM: Whoooo-wheeeeeee!

MARK: So after a few years of doing covers we started writing our own music. I think I was 17 when I wrote my first tune. We were playing up on Sunset Strip, mostly at Gazaris. I don't know if you remember that. It's where The Doors got started. Van Halen got started there. We were doing mostly cover tunes, and slowly but surely we weaned off the covers and were doing an all-original show. We were sharing the bill with these heavy metal bands, who were wild, getting into fights every night. Everybody thought we were so straight-laced, but we were a family and we dug it. We'd work Thursday through Sunday, three sets a night, all the way to 2:00 in the morning. We would go outside, waiting for our next set to come around . . . a scarf around the neck, sipping on Peppermint Schnapps or something to keep warm.

We were so young we really didn't know how to take care of ourselves. We were "singing on our youth," as they call it. You can only "sing on your youth" for so long. By Sunday you are so hoarse . . . you still have school Monday morning. It was really taking its toll. Then one night someone says, "Hey, let me buy you a drink!" And you're, like, "Oh, I've never done that before."

BM: How old were you then?

MARK: I was, like, 16 or 17. The clubs were, like, 18 and over, 21 and over. Some of them would say you have to stay back-stage because of our age. But after they got to know us they didn't care about that. The police never showed up, so I got to hang out with all these people. So one night . . . It's all, like, experimenting, and I'm not condoning experimenting . . . So you try drinking on the job once. First it gives you this false sense of happiness and this little security kind of thing. Then, after five or six songs into your set the alcohol starts to dry you out. So you start drying out, you start getting tired, and then you learn to . . . drink water!

Caffeine is a drug. Even sugar is a drug in some ways. It just weakens your whole thing. Drinking colas and even Gatorade can be unhelpful. It's been proven that eating good, and plenty of water, is the best thing.

And then as I got older, the cocaine scene came into play. I'm sure it was always around, but I don't think it was as readily available as it became when I was about 18. And finally, after years of being on the club scene, someone offered me some of that junk. And I rationalized to myself, "It's not alcohol, it's not marijuana," or whatever. So I tried cocaine, and that also gave me that false sense of security. I felt like I was on top of the world. I was hitting notes normally hit on my best days, and they were coming easily. But I didn't realize that I was doing more damage than good. But then a throat doctor told me that cocaine does what the throat sprays do that people use for soreness and hoarseness. It does numb your throat. But then you go to sing and you begin abusing your throat muscles and vocal chords and not even know it. That's what cocaine does. It kinda numbs you, gives you that false energy that makes you push yourself even higher, works for a second, but does so much more damage than good. It just doesn't work. It was so obvious from that very first that you don't mix drugs with performance if you want to last in this business.

BM: I've found that you can't mix drugs with anything, unless it's a little sugar in your coffee. But even too much coffee throws my performance off.

MARK: Even with the psychedelic drugs that seem to be on the rise again with a lot of the acid bands and the acid generation, with mushrooms, ecstasy, and stuff. I even dabbled in that. I remember we did this little gig. It was a cover gig that we were basically doing for fun. I went on a little psychedelic trip and totally forgot the lyrics. I was having a ball laughing all over the place but couldn't remember the words. And I said to myself, "You know what? This ain't working. People want to hear the words to this music."

So I'm not condoning drugs. I'm just saying, never mix drugs with performance if you want to be serious, have people take you seriously, and be consistent and professional in your performances.

Chapter 10

······················

Conversation Over!

What's the first thing a musician does when he or she signs a deal or a contract for a lucrative tour? Right! He or she starts spending money unnecessarily before being paid. We all do. We approach the good times as if they'll be with us forever. But guess what? They won't.

How many cats do you know who have had their cars repossessed or had to move out of that luxury condo after six months? Even more tragic: How many entertainers have you seen fall from their shaky pinnacle to the cheers of all those they abused on their way up?

A recent experience prompted me to write these notes as a reminder to all musicians. It is a scenario I've witnessed time and time again—talented players isolate themselves within their music and as a result tend to exhibit limited social skills (i.e., don't know how to deal with people), or show a total lack of common sense in dealing with their environment (i.e., don't know how to deal with business). I would say those two factors—not the music—are the primary causes of blocked entry to the music business and early exit from it.

Before I share that experience, let me clarify one important point. As artists, we are prone to many misconceptions. We struggle with our creations and often think we are the only ones working that riff, that melody, that lyric. Think again. Think of the thousands of groups and millions of musicians worldwide who are struggling to place those eight notes, those four beats, in some magical, never-before-heard order. As important as it is for your ego to say, "This music is worth sharing," as important as it is for you to feel that your music has credibility and meaning, it is equally important that you realize you ain't the only one doing it. You are one of millions of musicians out there with something to say. But in order to get to the next level, someone has to like you. I'm not talking about the butt-kiss syndrome, I'm just saying that someone has to like you—maybe not you personally, but you as a concept, as a possible money maker.

Don't think for a moment that you got the gig, the deal, or the tour solely because of your music. In fact, there are people who have been concerned about you, people who've been helping you, all along the way: the neighbors who didn't call the cops every night when you blew the roof off your garage practicing; the craftsman who fixed your axe for free when you were broke; the club owner who gave you your first shot; your girl-friend/boyfriend who busted her/his butt trying to manage the unmanageable.

When we as musicians—and as human beings—take a clear and honest look back, we will realize that we owe a lot of people. If this realization is forgotten, or goes unacknowledged, then as successful musicians we run the risk of thinking we got there by ourselves, owe no one anything, and can therefore treat everyone as we please.

You should also know that even successful bands have only a few years to make the really big bucks. After that, it's about trying to survive the trends and avoid being sucked into obscurity. It's the same on every high-stakes playing field, be it sports, entertainment, law, or Wall Street. When you are functioning in a minor-league money environment with a big-league lifestyle, the odds of longevity are slim to none.

If you are among the fortunate few who maintain star status down through the years, you must thank not only your talent, but your God and all the people who helped you get there. The point is, it is as important for you to maintain healthy relationships and use your resources wisely as it is to be a creative being. Which brings me to my story.

Two years ago, I was at a performance of a group that had just signed with a major label. They were doing the first of their promo gigs and I was backstage at the end of the concert. The vibe was high because it was a great performance. As I sipped my O'Doul's, I saw the lead singer shout to the old gentleman tending the VIP bar to bring him a m—f—g drink. It shocked me that this kid had the audacity to address an older gentleman in that manner. What the young singer didn't know was that the old gentleman had recorded numerous hits in the early days of rock and roll but, like so many others, had never righteously gotten paid. When I tried to explain to the young musician that this was no way to relate to anyone, he quickly reminded me that I could be a m—f—er, too. Conversation over!

Two months ago I saw that same young vocalist working behind the counter at Kinko's. He didn't remember me. As I paid him for my order, he accidentally referred to me as "man." I immediately reminded him that I was the man doing business with the company he worked for, and if he wanted to keep his present job, he'd best refer to me as "Mr. Mitchell." Conversation over! That's how quickly things change in this business.

Lonnie Jordan

Lonnie Jordan has played an important roll in the shaping of rock and roll. As one of the founders of War, he has garnered more gold and platinum than he can count. The group was at its peak during the 1970s and '80s. As a writer/producer/musician, Lonnie has participated in the creation and performance of some of the greatest hits of this era, such as "Low Rider," "Cisco Kid," and 'Why Can't We Be Friends." And now, as the sole original member of War, he carries the group and its music into the 21st century.

BM: Going back to the beginning, did you anticipate the level of success that you and the band would achieve? Did you think that War would become as big as it did?

LJ: Not at all. We started out playing around in clubs in West L.A., East L.A., Long Beach, and San Pedro, playing the blues circuit. From there we were just struggling to get a record deal. We're talking about 1961. I was a teenager wearing mascara over my lips like a mustache, and sideburns, so that I could look older. I don't call that paying dues. I was just young and having fun. Playing in clubs was exciting for me. Basically our dreams, not our goals, but our dreams . . . at that age we would all dream together. We had the same fantasies about seeing our names up in lights, on billboards and stuff, neon signs, night clubs . . . instead of the bands who were headlining. We wanted to see our names up there. But as we began to mature we started thinking about goals.

BM: How long did you guys play together between the time you started the group and your first record deal?

LJ: We never stopped. We always played venues. In 1968 we hooked up with Eric Burdon, the lead singer of the Animals. He fell in love with the group, and we ended up taking our act to England. That was the first time I set foot out of the United States. That's back when I met Jimmy Hendrix. I didn't know that it was Chas Chandler, from the group the Animals, was the one that brought Jimmy into the recording industry. That's why he and Eric were such good friends, because of that connection. Actually, England is where Jimmy's career started.

BM: That's kind of true for a lot of black artists.

LJ: Yeah! Tina Turner—the second half of her career took off in England. Actually, that's where we took off. The last night Jimmy played was with us at Ronnie Scott's. A lot of books that deal with the history of rock and roll skip over that. At the time people didn't know who War was. They just knew that Eric had a new group. People were saying, "Eric's got these Jamaican-Cuban, whoever these guys are." Where else could we come from? "They're from Africa, Antigua, or somewhere." They thought we were from everywhere except the United States. We had recorded our first song ("Spill the Wine") and it was just barely playing in the States. Nobody in England had heard it.

We got a lot of flak from the Africans in England when we cut the album *Black Man's Burden,* with Eric doing lyrics that spoofed the Queen. They thought we were Africans coming to England to start some kind of revolution. But when I made it clear that we were from a place called Compton, and went into my other act telling them how I felt about their politics, we didn't have any more trouble. But we only got flak from the Africans, which I thought was a little weird.

BM: There are a lot of transitions when entertainers make a lot of money fast. And you guys were from Compton, so I know you weren't used to handling a lot of cash. What did you do?

LJ: First of all, my first marriage—and I'd never put her down for my shortcomings—didn't work out. And this was a lady that was accustomed to nice things. So when it ended, I took a ride to the cleaners. I started spending money left and right.

BM: Why would you do that?

LJ: I started helping people, like friends that didn't have things that I had. Not only helping them, but I think it was to feed my ego too. I needed people to be around me, to party and keep indulging in all those things I knew I shouldn't have been doing. You know, the hard parties. I had two houses up in Bel Air that few people knew about. So I would be one person in one house and then I'd go to the other house and really party.

BM: All because you had the money?

LJ: Yeah! I had the money. I mean I had seven cars; Rolls Royces, Ferraris . . . I even had a Clinet when it first came out. I was living the life. I had a lot of other entertainers coming through that were all drugged out. We all did the same thing. We partied, and get up the next morning and start over. There was nothing else to do but go out and spend more money, or go to a club, or party some more.

BM: I really want to focus on this, because the issue is . . .

LJ: The issue is unhappiness. That's the bottom line.

BM: Unhappy? You had all this money. How were you unhappy?

LJ: That part of it I have never understood myself . . . except the fact that my personal life was unhappy and I had become my own worst enemy. I had no knowledge of how to deal with my personal life, so I looked for fulfillment outside of my marriage.

BM: So how does a young musician avoid this?

LJ: First of all, you avoid this by not doing anything that will hallucinate your mind. Keep a clear mind! Focus! If your mind is clean, your ass will follow, and you will not veer down that wrong road.

BM: But what do you do when you get all this money in your hands?

LJ: You put it away. And you don't give it to somebody to put away. If you don't know where to put it, you just hold onto it in a bank account until you get proper advice as to what to do with it. Even a bank, you have to be sure of. Give it to a major institution, and let it sit there for a minute until you learn what to do. People telling you to invest this, invest that . . . don't let your money out of your sight until you know where it's going to go and how it's going to turn over for you and what it's going to be for your retirement . . . and all that. And be careful of your friends.

BM: Friends—be careful of your friends? Talk to me about that!

LJ: Friends have a strange way of loving you. The word *love* comes in so many different fashions. The compliments that come out of the word *love* . . . when someone is sitting in front of you, indulging in your stuff, drinking your drinks, and how beautiful you are to that person at the moment. And as you're issuing, giving and giving from the heart because everybody's feeling so good, that's one love.

Then you have a whole other group of so-called friends that want to be around successful people. All that comes with the territory. But you know, I had major ups and downs, but I am not bitter and I don't point fingers at anyone. I had a great time and I don't regret it. I just thank God that I am alive today, alive and healthy, and I'm able to move on. Because I do not put the toxins in my body, thinking about the past. Because that is a disease, and I could be around here dead and just forget to lay down like a lot of musicians that have been through what we've been through.

BM: Did you think the money would never end?

LJ: I knew something had to end. I didn't really focus on the money at all. I was running around in jeans spending money on dumb stuff. But the music had to end because there were a lot of bad things going on. Everything ended in 1980. I was totally, flat broke. Lawsuits up the yang-yang. When "T" and I got married I got away from music totally and began living a normal life. It really put me back in orbit and made me realize where I was at. I became more creative musically, because I had a chance to start over again.

So I put a whole 'nother group together. I had to go through the whole court thing over the name, because I stayed clean and focused, cleaned up my act, and said, "There's no reason why we should let the people down."

Chapter 11

....

Time Keeps
on Tickin'

I hope that you don't think of time as merely
something the rhythm section is responsible for. It is certainly that, but the beat goes beyond any musical function. Time
is clearly a dimension through which melody and harmony
flow. It is also an element that measures how much control
you have of yourself and your environment. If you are aware
of the broader meaning of time, you are probably a good
musician and an organized individual; if you are unaware of
time, you are probably the undependable type who consistently creates problems in every situation. By *unaware* I mean
you can't seem to get to the gig on time, or in enough time
to function in a relaxed manner—you operate in a haze,
stressed out, discombobulated. The band worries that you
may not show, the club manager worries the band may not
start on time, and the audience has to sit and watch you set
up and tune up.

How can you be late to a gig? You have at least 20 hours to prepare for it. The gig is your job, your livelihood, your reason for being. How can you be late? You are not out fighting wars or discovering new planets When you get up in the morning, you should already be planning how to get to the gig. Working on your car, visiting your kids, shopping for your mom—these are all important functions, but have nothing to do with the gig.

Musicians are known to have an extensive supply of lame excuses and, in many cases, a disturbing disregard for time. The quickest way to be denied a bank loan is to put *musician* on the application, because our credit worthiness is about one notch above that of snake oil salesmen. If you can't get to the gig on time, how can you be expected to take care of the rest of your business on time? Some musicians think it's cool to run in at the last minute. It's not! In days past, when musicians had two and three gigs or sessions a day, that kind of behavior was tolerated. However, those days are gone.

When you disrespect time, you jeopardize your music as well as your reputation. Time is an elusive little monster, often creating the illusion that more of it exists than actually does. It can make you rush or it can make you drag. It can make you put off doing things until that chore is no longer in your mind. If you do not master time, it will run away with you. When you play with someone who rushes, you have to lay in the pocket; when you play with someone who drags, you may have to play "on top" just to keep the pulse and energy where it should be. You have to give time more than it asks for. If you calculate that it will take 15 minutes to get to the gig, give yourself half an hour or more.

Here are some basic warning signals to be aware of when

working in new situations: Watch out when a musician shows up two minutes before hit time with an attitude, with friends, hungry, or all of the above. This is someone who does not honor time, the gig, or you. This is someone who doesn't realize that his or her attitude toward the gig is a reflection of an attitude toward life. It is important to master time not only for your music but also for your career. Instead of always playing catch-up because you're operating from a time deficit, make time your friend—it will work for you.

Bobby
Rodriguez

A Grammy-nominated recording artist, Bobby Rodriguez is a gifted musician/composer and producer. He has earned one gold and three platinum records while recording and performing with such greats as Quincy Jones, Lalo Schiffrin, Herbie Hancock, and Ray Charles, to name a few. Although he tours constantly with his own band, he has always shown concern for the musical future of children, performing hundreds of musical education concerts a year. He is president of the Hispanics Musician Association, a member of the Board of Governors of the National Academy of Recording Arts & Sciences and a member of the Institute for the Preservation of Jazz, and he teaches at the Los Angeles County High School for the Arts and Pasadena City College.

BM: Let's talk about time: the relationship between developing good time in your music and getting to work on time.
BR: Time is everything—the time to practice, the time to make sure that your mind is set up so that you're ready to play your gig, the time for music and musical interactions, and the time to be on time for whatever it is that you are intending to do. This allows other people to feel good about you because you are, in fact, responsible enough to respect their time as well. In

music, of course, the most important element *is* time. Without time, rhythm is just chaos.

BM: How do you ensure that your musicians will show up on time?

BR: Try to pay a good salary. The older I become, the more I realize that money is a great motivator. You try to keep everything on a schedule, but you build your value on faith and trust. You trust that your musicians will be at a certain place at a certain time. And they trust that you will pay them, that this job will be a place where they can feel good about themselves and do what you have practiced to do. Money is not always the answer, but it is a good, respectful place to begin.

BM: Have you had musicians that were very important to your program that had problems doing things in a timely manner?

BR: I remember my first teacher, Mr. Bill Taggert, way back in elementary school, gave me something that has always stuck with me. He said, "The greatest musician in the world has no value at all if they don't show up for the gig." If the guy is wonderful in rehearsal, adding to your personal confidence, and it feels great, and then all of a sudden he's late, or doesn't show up to the gig, or disrespectful, making the job uncomfortable, I've learned to eliminate that person and move on. Because it's all about having fun.

BM: Right now you are in Latin jazz, but you've played everything. As a teacher, how do you encourage your students to develop a good sense of time?

BR: Number one . . . listening and playing along with records. I think that's very important. If a drummer wants to play bebop, then he should play along with some Blakey and the Jazz Messengers . . . whether you know the breaks or the stops is immaterial. It's important to get a feel for someone you like and play along with them on a record. Get the emotion, the spirit, the rhythm, the time . . . and just go with it.

As a teacher, I'm not trying to develop musicians per se. I'm trying to develop young people who have respect for the art form, for the artist that they might become, or support in years to come. I'm also developing an audience. A very small percentage of students will ultimately become professional musicians. I teach my students that they have to keep their options open. The great musicians of today are not just musicians. They are personalities, performers, entertainers, and they also go into other areas . . . writers, composers, arrangers, video makers . . . whatever the business will bear and whatever they're good at. And every area has the possibility of income.

These are the kind of young people that I want to invest in. And this is the kind of musician that I want to play with—upwardly thinking, aggressive, mobile musicians who are positive and doing something other than sitting around all day waiting for the phone to ring. I tell my kids all the time, "If you're sitting there waiting by the phone, you're waiting for nothing." Go out and make something happen! You have to be the motivating factor.

BM: But how do you teach responsibility?

BR: I hold my students to the highest standards possible. The standards of the recording industry, studio musician standards, which are: Be in your place one-half hour to 45 minutes early, totally prepared: music, instrument, clothing if there's going to be a visual, happy. Bring a good attitude so that you can contribute not just musically but spiritually.

Chapter 12

....

Recording a Disaster

Many musicians are overcome with joy and anticipation at the prospect of recording their music—especially when it's the first time. As time goes on, the excitement wears off. You come to realize that it is just the first step of a long, often-frustrating journey.

I'm very fortunate to have had the opportunity to be around some great producers. With each experience I tried to learn as much as I could about what works and what doesn't in terms of getting the best performance possible. For example, when I worked with blues great Willie Dixon, I learned simplicity, how to produce music for the common ear. Every producer has his/her method. There is something to be learned from all of them.

But some truths apply to any successful recording session. I'm reminded of a studio experience that broke every rule of thumb and was a total disaster. I have to take responsibility for that fiasco because, as producer, I should have set the ground rules from the beginning, and I didn't. I turned down that heavily trod path of assumption: I assumed the artist understood the process . . . and he didn't.

I arrived for the eight o'clock session at seven o'clock so that I would have plenty of time to kick back and make sure everything was in order. Eight o'clock came . . . no artist. I had just been hired to produce this session, and I had told the artist's manager to get there early so we could discuss direction. At 8:20 PM they arrived, not just the artist, but his whole entourage, which consisted of his buddies, their girlfriends, and a host of groupies.

They had what amounted to a portable bar with a variety of drinks and various unmentionables. The artist was dressed in an outfit that would have made Kiss take note. This group was ready to party. They had come to watch their boy cut a hit record. The only thing he seemed interested in was getting to the mic and doing his thing in front of his friends. We hadn't even started, and they had already broken all of my rules:

- **He was late.** Recording requires concentration and composure. You have to arrive in plenty of time to focus your thoughts on the performance.

- **He brought guests.** If you're not directly related to the recording, you shouldn't be in the studio. Friends, family, and investors will be more of a distraction than an inspiration. As a producer, seeing someone frown could make me think that I had missed hearing something, when in reality that person's thoughts could be a thousand miles away.

- **He was dressed for a party, not for work.** Dress comfortably for work—this is not a concert. You may have to do your part over and over. You may have to stand in front of that mic all night, so you need to be comfortable.

- **He arrived too late for us to discuss direction.** You have to take time to discuss what you want. You must relate to the engineer or producer or whoever is responsible for your sound.

Then the fun began. Because I hadn't been specific with the manager, I felt obligated to deal with things as they were. As we began working the vocals, it became obvious that this singer didn't have a clue. He was performing, not recording, and reacting to the shouts of encouragement from his entourage, totally disregarding the position of the mic. It was slowly becoming a drunken circus, which meant that they broke my final rule:

- **No booze, no drugs, no nothing:** Even too much coffee will make you speed ahead of "the groove."

In a desperate attempt to save the session I stopped the music and sent the engineer out. I announced that we were going to break and that the party was to be moved to the manager's house. I told the artist to go home and put on some workclothes (sweats) and come back prepared to work. That didn't sit well with some members of his entourage. But I wasn't concerned about them. The project and my professionalism were more important. He soon returned, and we managed to get a few tunes done. I think he was surprised at how much better his performance was without the distractions. But that didn't close the rift created by my decisions. They didn't call me to complete the project, which actually was a good thing.

A year later, I ran into the singer at a party and asked him about the project. As you might expect, it was never completed. He wasted all of the investors' money on studio time and *producers*.

And when the money's gone and the "good times" end, you know, "they don't hang around anymore." I couldn't feel much sympathy for the guy because this is something we see every day . . . millions of dollars wasted by artists trying to produce themselves without seeking the ears and experience of some-one who could help make their dream a reality.

It is impossible for an artist to know what he or she really sounds like. When I produce my projects, I listen to the musicians and often depend on them for advice. I think that when you record with an open mind, and surround yourself with people that you can trust, you have a good chance of coming up with something good.

I guess there are many ways to evaluate various situations. The first measure I use to determine whether I want to deal with something is hygienic: How clean is the scene? Whether it be a restaurant, a car, or a date, if it ain't clean, it ain't happenin'. When I'm looking for a good recording studio, the first thing I check out is the bathroom. That's right, the toilet! If the bathroom is funky, chances are the condition of the studio is going to be funky. If cleanliness is next to godliness, and your music is sacred to you, the two should go hand in hand. If music is the most important thing in your life, the conditions under which you record your music, whether it be commercial or personal, should be the best you can afford. You should strive to get the best recording possible.

Clean is my thing. I realize that it's not everybody's thing. But I assure you that a clean and organized approach will work to your advantage. Whether it is clean and organized charts, a clean and organized rehearsal, or clean and organized directions to the gig, it will always be to your advantage. Remember, too, that there are personality types that thrive on disorganization. That's where they feel comfortable, because there is seemingly less pressure in disorganization. Duh! The goal is good music, and you're going to reach it more quickly with a clean and organized approach.

Nowhere is this more necessary than in a recording studio.

Whether it's a home session, a project room, or a big commercial studio, money is wasted if the wrong choices are made. Millions of dollars are wasted when musicians choose a pricey studio for a project that could be done on an eight-track or choose a "demo" studio for compositions and arrangements that require more sophisticated equipment. Often decisions are made based on a shortage of time or money. Allow me to present a few considerations that are often ignored.

- **Check out the liability insurance.** Make sure the place you spend your money to work in and store your tapes at provides you with a minimum amount of coverage. Suppose you trip on loose cords and bust your head, erasing that killer melody you were about to lay out. Suppose the studio goes up in flames, or down in an earthquake, and destroys your masters. These are unlikely scenarios, but still possibilities. What recourse do you have?

- **Check out your studio at length.** Take your time and talk to the people who work there. I don't mean that you should become a pain in the butt with a lot of trivial questions. If possible, observe the engineer in session and see how he or she works. There are many types of engineers, including those who do exactly what you tell them to do (even when they know it won't work), those who become the "producer" and want to tell you how to do it, those who allow interruptions and take telephone calls during the sessions (usually in the middle of a groove), and those who are constantly in a state of emergency, trying to figure out why something on the board doesn't work. Try to find an engineer who knows the board, has experience with your kind of music, has energy and a good vibe, and is concerned about what you want. (Then call me with his or her phone number.)

- **Make a real close inspection of the mixing board.** If you notice water rings from glasses and beer bottles, cigarette ashes, dust—any sign that the board has not been tended to—you can anticipate trouble. If there are wrappers, papers, sections of tape, or other trash scattered around the room, you can anticipate trouble. Usually the inside of the board will be like the outside. Even if their hourly rate seems really good, with the probable delays and interruptions, you'll end up losing time and money—not to mention the groove.

- **Find out who has recorded there and what other clients they have worked with.** One thing to remember is that most good studios don't have to do a lot of advertising. Their business is based on referrals—word of mouth. When I say a good studio, I don't mean expensive. A good studio will give you what you need at a price you can afford.

If your project is the most important thing in your career, you should place the quality of the studio above the hourly rate. Take all the time you need to get the quality that will allow you to compete in the music marketplace.

Robyn Whitney and Michael McDonald
(Private Island Trax Recording Studio, L.A.)

Robyn Whitney

Robyn Whitney has headed up Private Island Trax
Recording Studio for the past 14 years. Along with husband/master engineer, Michael McDonald, they have developed Trax into the most successful budget studio in Southern California. The studio deals with all phases of recording that include sound services for film and TV, mastering being their specialty. Their project/client list reads like a who's who of the entertainment business.

BM: When and how did you get into the recording business?

RW: This studio has existed for 17 years and I've been here for 14. Prior to that I was in New York City. I was Diana Ross's assistant for several years. And before that I was with the management company that handled Kiss, The Isley Brothers, Chaka Khan . . . people like that. Before that I was with Warner Brothers. So I've seen the management and the legal and promotional side. I've been on the inside of the contracts and decision making. So this was kind of an obvious place for me when I came back home to L.A.

BM: How did you get drawn into the studio business itself?

RW: I had worked in PR and I had also worked in special events, where you're coordinating a lot of different things. People tend to have an "event attitude" toward the studio sometimes. They're about to start a big event in their lives. It's very costly, and often they've been planning many years for this. So having that enthusiasm for them and having that sense of organization is very important to running a studio. I knew the owner from when he was a player, and we had talked down through the years. He was going crazy trying to run the studio without any help, and he just offered me the job out of the blue.

BM: Let's approach the first side of this discussion, the first side being some of the obvious things that musicians do that create problems when they come into a studio.

RW: A musician coming into the studio without a producer is always a problem. The musician rarely understands the need for a good producer. They're playing their instrument. They see the trees, they don't see the whole forest. A lot of them don't have a plan in mind as to how they're going to get this finished record into the hand of someone who can do something with it. They're unclear on how to step outside of themselves and make rational decisions about the very emotional business of music. Often they come to us expecting us to hold their hands through this process, and it's not our obligation, as much as we'd like to help them. They become highly dependent on the engineer when they don't have a producer. The engineer will often feel compelled to help them, as a good human being. But he really can't, because legally we are not supposed to make comments in the creative area. As a studio we deal only with the sonics. Creative decisions are not for the engineer. That's what you need a producer for.

BM: My understanding has always been that in the early days of recording, the engineer *was* the producer. There was no such thing as a producer. When did all of that change?

RW: The more intense the technology got, the more you needed a specialized guy who could concentrate on the recording and another guy who could concentrate on the record. And they are two different things. If you step inside any good control room these days, it looks like the inside of a jet plane. There are more knobs and things and toys to know about. There are four-year college degrees offered by your top colleges just to train a beginning engineer. Then they need a year or so of internship before they even assist an engineer. It is such an all-consuming job, both in preparation for it and the actuality of it.

A producer is just a different cat. He's a guy who's been studying music real hard and he may know something technically. But he's not somebody who's going to reach over and adjust the reverb. He's a guy who has to say, "Hold on! I think we lost the groove around bar four." And then he turns to the engineer and says, "Roll it back!" The engineers that I know who are producers never engineer for themselves when they're producing. It would be like trying to be a head surgeon and a foot surgeon on the same patient at the same time.

Musicians working on their own projects without a producer are rarely prepared accordingly. Half the time they show up with no charts. Sometimes they come underrehearsed. They thought they were well rehearsed because they were limited by their own musical knowledge. And had they been in the hands of a good producer, they might have been kept in the rehearsal a couple of more weeks until they had worked out all the kinks they were now struggling with on studio time.

Another problem is created when musicians allow their emotions to override reality. Often they're convinced that because it only took three hours to play through the whole album in rehearsal, that's how much time it will take in the studio. Like the guy who called and said, "I have a song that's only three minutes long. So could I just book ten minutes?" Musicians just don't see that whole picture unless they've had a lot of session experience. There's nothing to say that musicians can't become good producers, as long as they study and truly work at it. Working without a producer is like flying a trapeze without a net. You expect the studio to be the net, and we just can't do that.

BM: What is the producer's role, from beginning to end?

RW: Michael McDonald, the producer who owns this studio, described the producer as a person who wears three hats. You have to keep a grip on the business end (How do we market? How is the image? Who's going to buy this?), the budget—all the administrative stuff (if they have a record deal, union wages, contributions, the time in the studio, is the budget a little padded for the end?). Record labels want all that to be handed to them complete. They don't want to do anything.

Hence, the all-end deal, where the label gives the entire budget to the producer and says, "Do the project anyway you choose, but if it goes over budget it comes out of your pocket."

The next part of it is that you have to have developed ears and be able to stand outside of the individual instruments and hear the whole thing, compare it to what's in the marketplace, catch the things that aren't working and eliminate them. A producer has to be a good musician.

And the third part is psychiatry. You may be a great businessman and musician, but if you don't know how to get the best performance from the singer—who's coming unglued and crying and freaking out—the production is going nowhere. It's the business of hand holding and encouraging and being the cheerleader and coach at the same time . . . knowing how to make people relax and give it their best.

BM: I've mentioned choosing a good engineer. What kind of problems do you have when it comes to artist/engineer relationships?

RW: There are engineers who desperately want to be producers. And if they get too emotionally attached to an artist's work, if they truly love this kind of music and really want to be in there kickin' and doin' it, little problems can pop up now and then. They start to pass opinions. They start to step into the producer's arena by making comments and suggestions . . . and they absolutely cannot do it. An engineer should never have an opinion outside of the best way to get the best recording. He's the second set of ears. The first set is the client's. Engineers who step into the creative arena frustrate themselves, alienate the client, and eventually get their asses fired!

Chapter 13

....

It's Your Thing

Not long ago, during one of my gigs at a jazz spot in Los Angeles, I was handed a note while I was playing. The note advised me that one of the top music reviewers in the business was sitting in the audience directly in front of me. I struggled to maintain my composure. Why was I freaking out? Why were my hands beginning to turn to putty and my concentration breaking up? I've been in this situation many times and always survived. Why was I so nervous this time? Besides being caught by surprise, I had also been playing material that I wasn't totally familiar with, and I'm sure I sounded a little tentative. But I think that after reading this reviewer's column for years, the serious critiques and analysis of many great performers, I was a little unnerved and intimidated by his presence.

It was only through many years of performing that I learned to create and maintain a positive facade (most of the time, anyway), even when everything around me felt shaky. These are defining moments that determine where a gigger is coming from. In that moment, I had to decide what my purpose was. Was I going to suddenly make some kind of musical statement in order to impress this critic? Would I keep the audience number one and continue doing the things that they came to hear? Would I focus on the music and give the performance all I could give? Or would I divert the attention to the sidemen in hopes that their musicianship would carry me? I had done all of these things in the past, but I decided that this time it would be different.

As time began to slow to a crawl, I tried to set up my approach. I glanced toward the critic, but he was looking upward, listening, absorbing every note, every phrase. I thought, "Tonight I don't stand a chance." In those brief moments, so many things became clear to me. I realized how turned off I am when I see musicians change their whole thing when other musicians come on the scene. Not only is it amateurish, but it exposes an obvious insecurity that is noticeable to everyone, especially a music critic. I had to continue working the audience, because no matter what the reviewer might think of my technique, I'd score a lot more points if I had the house rockin'. I had to focus on the music while maintaining my rapport with the audience. Hiding behind other musicians is a form of wimping out and is unacceptable, especially when you're a leader.

And so, in the final hour, I was left with one choice: Be myself and go for it. And in that moment of extreme anxiety, I decided to sidestep out of the comfort zone and do something that was impromptu, fresh, and fun. I decided to sing a tune. This in itself may not seem like a big deal, unless you realize the stark fear that has always gripped me at the very thought of singing. Never having been able to escape the devastation suffered as the result of an audience that reacted to my first vocal offering as if it were a comedy act, I had avoided singing at all costs. I had even convinced myself that I was incapable of learning lyrics.

So why would I play my weakest hand at such a critical point? Because sometimes we have to break our pattern and do the unexpected. The point is that we often take our music too seriously. We become so intent on our approach that our music becomes burdensome to the audience, and we lose our sense of fun. I have always tried to stay in familiar territory so that I could feel comfortable in my performance. But that comfort too often translates into boredom for the band, a dull predictability for the audience, and an uninspired performance from me.

But why would I risk artistic suicide when my ability was under such scrutiny? It's like jumping into water over my head to learn how to swim, that first step out of the plane on a first parachute jump, asking the object of my affection for that first date, or my first bold step into the ice dip after the first work-out at the gym. It's all reckless abandon. It's all jumping into the water in order to erase all options except swimming. It's flirting with the point of no return in the middle of uncharted water.

I took a deep breath, tried to clear my head, and dove into the lyrics. As the words miraculously flowed forth, my confidence welled up and I actually began to enjoy the tune. After the set, I mingled with the audience and carefully made my way toward the critic as he was getting ready to leave. I spoke with him only briefly but tried to expose as much information about myself as courtesy would allow. The following day I woke up to the best review I have ever received. As I read it, it became clear that the reviewer was focusing on me as a whole artist, not just as a piano player. He wrote about the family atmosphere that I created with the audience, the young musician I allowed to perform as a guest, the lightness in which I approached my singing.

What this writer reinforced for me is the importance of covering all facets of the presentation. You have to cover your band, your music, your audience, and, most of all, yourself. It is only through your fulfillment that a spirit of joy can flow through your music and uplift your audience.

Gary
Mallaber

Gary Mallaber is one of the most prolific recording drummers in the business. His discography is a who's who of the pop-rock world—from Bruce Springsteen, Steve Miller, Van Morrison, the Beach Boys, Peter Frampton, Pete Seger, and Bonnie Raitt to Barbra Streisand, Cher, and countless others. He has taken the immeasurable store of information that he has gathered through the years and become one of the business's most versatile producer/arrangers. When not touring with one of the many top groups who keep him busy, he is in the studio working on something new.

BM: When did you get started?

GM: I got started when I was about 6 or 7 years old. I was a product of a very musical environment. In Buffalo during those years, you had every special form of music coming at you at the same time. The best of blues, R&B, jazz, and the beginnings of rock and roll were all spewing forth at the same time.

BM: But when did it become personal?

GM: I was taking private drum lessons at about 6 and on up through high school. I was influenced by every piece of music that came at me.

BM: Do you remember your first professional gig?

GM: Oh yeah! I was about 12 years old and we played at a birthday party for somebody. I think I made $7.50, and that was a big deal for us. And before I knew it I was 15 and playing in a house band. But that was an era when there were plenty of places to execute what you had learned. That's the advantage we had, being able to play five and six nights a week.

BM: So youngsters now spend a lot of time in their garages practicing. There doesn't seem to be as much opportunity as there should be to play in a big city like L.A.

GM: But if you go outside of the city, I think you may come across many more opportunities to play a normal gig.

BM: In the smaller towns, that's where a lot of the music is coming from!

GM: It is! Well, technology has changed and it has enabled you to stay at home and record. Before, everyone would have to go to the big city because that's where all the recording machines were. And now you've got all of that under your fingertips for the price of a small car . . . or less.

BM: I know you have produced a lot of groups. Were you in your early producer stage when you played with Van Morrison?

GM: I was working in New York City with a group that had been signed to CBS. And off of that I met Van Morrison. He was playing in a little folk club. To make a long story short, I offered my services, and a few months later we started rehearsing this record which was to become *Moon Dance*.

BM: Were you actually giggin' with him at the time?

GM: We were gigging a little bit. It was a little raggedy, a little haphazard. This was prior to the time when the singer-songwriter began getting the recognition. It was always the band, or the group, or the event. When the singer-songwriter began getting his due, the whole scene changed forever. Off of these records with Van Morrison, because he was such an icon in the rock world, opened up a lot of doors for me. I did six albums with Van.

BM: The most notable being *Moon Dance*. I've played that many times.

GM: It's ironic how that happened. Here we were recording in New York City, running up to Woodstock, where Van was living, to rehearse. We were putting all these tunes together. And in the midst of all these semi-folk-rock tunes and rock beats that we were doing at the time, and even some little R&B things, there was this song that he started playing on the acoustic guitar. I had hardly ever worked with an acoustic guitar . . . it was always electric.

BM: The original recording has a swing feel. How did you come up with that?

GM: We started churning out this little tune, experimenting and playing with it. We started turning the rhythm around. And before we knew it we had this swing, bebop pattern for *Moon Dance*, right in the midst of all this rock.

BM: So you went totally outside of your groove and came up with a huge hit?

GM: We didn't have a problem trying something different because it felt natural. At the time it was recognized by the critics. But the entirety of *Moon Dance*—the record, the album, the single—never received the accolades that it is now receiving, and we're more than 20-some years down the road. That just goes to show you what kind of odd cycles we come in and out of in the music world. I remember when we were on the bill with Black Sabbath. Here we were, in the midst of all this metal, playing this jazz tune, if you wanted to label it that. But it had to be that. It really couldn't be anything but what that was. We went right to it.

BM: You know some of the trends. You're producing a lot of the young acts. What do you say to them as far as developing a healthy attitude?

GM: The first thing I try to do is to make them find out who they are. If it's pleasant or painful . . . we don't know how that's going to turn out. This is aside from your song writing, technique, or playing ability. Most of the time I hear bands that can play good individually. But what it becomes when they play as a band is the crux of the whole thing. You have to find out, without emulating other people. You may discover as you write that, hmm, I don't write big and heavy. I write very emotionally. I write ballads. I write close. So I try to make these guys deal with this. Lets find out who we are. It may be very different.

Chapter 14

· ·

Just a Casual?

I'm sure you've noticed people will say just about anything to get what they want—or think they need: "I love you," "A piece of cake," "The check's in the mail," and "Trust me" are but a few of the classic lines tossed your way when someone wants something from you. The effect of these little dictums can be measured in degrees, from gentle persuasion to outright lies. I think the most aggravating situation for a musician is, after taking a gig booked as "just a little background music," to arrive with the band and realize the scale of the gig is more like a coronation—but you've only charged for "just a little background music."

Several years ago, an agent booked me for a Wednesday night private party, explaining that it was a small event with a few people coming in from out of town. Although the gig was at a pretty ritzy hotel, I took it as another casual—until I got there. The room at the hotel turned out to be the grand ballroom. As we made our way to the stage area, we were passed by an army of caterers. A nervous platoon of acolytes worked feverishly on grand flower arrangements. A string-and-harp ensemble was setting up for cocktails. A champagne fountain bubbled with pink champagne. And the tables were set in sterling silver, with place settings for more than a hundred people. This was no casual. This was an extravaganza. An event. A spectacle.

We had been screwed. Overcome with terrible thoughts of what I was going to do to the agent, my trance was interrupted when the bass player bumped my arm and asked, "How much did you say this gig paid?" My lips could not form the words to voice the amount. I was embarrassed, humiliated, and furious. How could my band believe I had taken this gig for this amount of money? They would suspect me of screwing with the money like I knew the agent was doing. Oh, and yes, the "folks" flying in from out of town were members of a royal family from the Middle East. Hello!

I had been duped. It took everything I had to muster the professionalism expected of me. The guests were there to have a good time, and that was our responsibility. We had been screwed, not just by the unscrupulousness of the agent, but by my negligence: I hadn't taken the time to ask the right questions. Had I carried on a little dialogue, I might have exposed the fact that this was far more than "just a little gig," and we would have entered into some serious negotiations. Had I known the dynamics of this royal event, I would have insisted on "royal bread."

I did remedy the situation by not working for that agency again. As a matter of fact, I very rarely work for agents on the local level. For musicians who don't mind lining agents' pockets, the agent/artist arrangement is OK—they need to work. As for me, I would rather apply that extra effort to developing my own clientele, my own gigs. It's a lot of work. Agents have to work their butts off too. They have a lot of time and money to recoup. That doesn't justify taking 40–50% of my money from a gig. Historically, legally, and ethically, 10–20% is standard. Anything beyond that should be discussed.

Unfortunately, extreme as I tend to be sometimes, I didn't just start asking questions, I turned into the grand inquisitor, asking questions musicians don't usually ask, like "How much is the client *really* paying for the band?" As might be expected, most agents don't like to do business with me, or with any other musician who insists on being treated fairly. Here again, you need to establish what kind of musician you're going to be.

You have a choice in determining what kind of gigger you want to be. You can choose to take anything that is offered to you no matter what the conditions are. You can gig for the sake of gigging, for steady income, for personal development or just for fun. Or you can approach this as a serious career that you are trying to establish and take each and every gig as an opportunity to move to another level (you never know who's sitting in the audience). When it comes to your gig, ask questions: How many miles? Is there complimentary parking/meals? Who is the contact person at the event? Who exactly is sponsoring the event? Try to get a clear picture of the event. Only then will you be able to determine if you are being offered the right amount of money. Only then will you be able to begin to establish what kind of gigger you are choosing to be.

Susan DeBois

Susan DeBois' journey in the area of artist
representation began when she became part owner of a
French restaurant in Culver City, California, during the 1980s.
During a very difficult period she was approached by another
club, one that was closing, and asked if she would take their
music showcase. They came to her restaurant and built a stage,
and she went out and bought a PA system. As the popularity of
the club grew, so did the need for new entertainment. She soon
found herself going out, reviewing acts, and negotiating with
them to come to her club. That's how it all began. DeBois,
through her DeBois Productions, is one of the most active
artist reps in the country, working for the high-end corporate
market, celebrity weddings, and events.

BM: Sometimes musicians and agencies fail to get complete
and often crucial information about gigs. How does that happen?

SD: It should never happen! The musician should get all necessary information beforehand, or the agency is not doing its
job. They need to know the location, time, dress, what time
they can load in, where and how do they park. And that's just
how to get to the gig. And then the band should have a complete and written-out timeline of what is expected. If it's a wedding, they have to know when to announce the bride and

groom, the first dance, the toast, etc. All this information is critical. The more information you can give to the band, the better job they're going to do for the client. It's on the agent to get that info, but it's *also* on the musician to make sure he/she has it.

If that stuff hasn't been given to him then he or she should find out why. The musicians should have their own checklist. It's up to the bandleader to make sure that he/she and the sidemen have the proper information.

BM: Do agencies have problems getting complete information for their events? And if so, what are some of the more consistent problems?

SD: Yes, a lot of times we do have to fight to get information.

We often find problems, not from the clients, but when we have to work with various party planners. Party planners have a tendency to withhold information on some occasions, being that it might be a celebrity or someone important. and there's certain stuff they just don't want you to know. Often they have too much on their plate, they're not organized, and by the time they get the info to you it's too late.

BM: What's the reason for withholding information from the agent?

SD: Control . . . somebody is in control! The planners I choose to work with . . . I never have that problem. If I do, it's just too difficult to do the job. And that just doesn't interest me. There are some phenomenal planners in the business. But unfortunately many of them do not know the nuances between serving music and serving food. I think that my having owned a nightclub enables me to realize the connection so that we can establish a real flow for everyone concerned.

There's a lot of timing involved in this—for example, the kitchen, during an event. They have hot food that they have to get out. And if the band is doing some wild, upbeat dance right at that point, the band is not doing their job. In other words, you can't be self-indulgent. Yes, you want to make a great party. Absolutely! It's critical that you make a great party and they deserve a great party. Timing is most important.

BM: Besides being aware of the tempo of the event, how else can the band enhance the flow?

SD: You should work closely with the banquet manager, because they're the ones who can tell you when, where, and how. The first thing to do is to introduce yourself as soon as you arrive. That's important as a bandleader. As a sideman it's important to watch your cues.

And for private homes especially, you need specific load-in information. Are there stairs, concrete, grass, steep grades?

What do you have to deal with in order to give your musicians enough time for a comfortable load-in. That's one of the things that you want to know. Is this event in a banquet facility or a private home? We actually have a clause in our contracts that states that there may be an additional fee for difficult or early load-ins. We also have a checklist that we send to each client letting them know how much power is needed. How many stairs are there? When do the catering trucks arrive? What's the closest access to the stage area? The bandleader has to also take it upon himself to attend to a lot of that.

BM: I always scream about not getting a full description of the job I've been hired to do. Why is that always a problem?

SD: Often planners choose not to tell us who their clients are, thinking that in that way nobody can get into trouble. I work with one of the major planners in the city, who actually helped to build my career. So I have only the best things to say about this guy. But even with that, I once had a terribly embarrassing situation. As things turn out, I'm scheduled to do this big event but I don't have a clue who it's for. I get a call two days before the event from a guy who says, "Hi! I'd like to sing a song with the band at Charlie Sheen's wedding and I'd like to speak with the keyboard player. And, will we have time to rehearse?" He starts asking me all these questions. I said, "I'm not doing Charlie Sheen's wedding." He said, "Excuse me, but is this DeBois Productions?" I said, "Yes, this is Susan DeBois." "Then you're doing Charlie's wedding this Saturday," he retorted. I was totally embarrassed. I had none of that information. The planner and I entered into serious conversation about the issues of trust. And I let him know that I must have all pertinent information in order to do my job.

BM: What are your words to musicians as far as dealing with agencies?

SD: First of all, it's a team effort between agent and band leader, and we have to work as a team. The agent needs to get you all the information that we can possibly get. The musician has to execute everything the way it is supposed to be executed. It's not about you. It's not about me. It's about the client. It's about making them as happy as possible. The deal is that the big companies and hotels are not comfortable working directly with the bandleader. They want the umbrella of an agency that has eight or ten bands on its roster. If a singer gets sick or a leader gets sick, it's covered. The agency has the resources to back it up.

Number two—and I know that agents are definitely resented in the music community because it's thought that we make so much money—musicians aren't aware of our gigantic overhead. Just one employee . . . you're talking 40,000 a year, plus benefits. Do the math! We need that help so that we can have all the resources to provide you with all the work that you need. So musicians need to stop looking at agents like they are the enemy and work at creating a team effort so that everyone can work more on a regular basis, with no hassles or egos involved. If we can achieve that, we have free sailing and we can get more and more work.

A good agency will not look at the musicians like they are doing them a favor. No matter what percentage of work the agent is providing, the agent is nothing without the musician. We are only as good as the musicians who are working with us. It's important that the word gets out to the agencies that they have to treat their musicians with total respect at all times. We are of that consciousness. We also realize that we have to do the best we can by the client, so we're tough. We enforce our rules and expect our musicians to do the positive. And I feel that if you are a good musician, a professional musician, that's not even a thought.

Gigging Checklist

· ·

The following is a checklist (provided by DeBois Productions) on the do's and the don'ts for the casual gig experience. Much of it can easily be applied to formal gigs in general—and, yes, to life itself. Although it is assumed that all agents and planners are aware of these particulars, it is suggested that bandleaders make this information available to their musicians before an event (new musicians or those that need reminding).

- **CODE OF DRESS:** A clean, pressed, black tuxedo (not off-black or dark blue) with a clean, pressed white tuxedo shirt. A black cummerbund and a black bow tie (unless otherwise specified). Refer to: *Gig*, May 1997

- **STANDARDS OF COURTESY:** Maintain a high level of friendly, courteous, polite, and fun-loving behavior toward management, coordinators, and personnel as well as each other. If you have a problem, take a deep breath, and speak directly to your bandleader. Remember that tact goes a long way. Refer to: *Gig*, December 1997, April 1998

- **THERE IS NO EXCUSE FOR LATENESS:** Take care of your vehicles during the week (gas, oil, tires, etc.) to eliminate problems on the weekends. Leave early enough to be able to deal with any emergency. All musicians should be ready and in position 15 minutes prior to downbeat. All musicians should have the bandleader's beeper number Refer to : *Gig*, September 1997, May 1998

- **INTERMISSION AND BREAKS:** Musicians do not mingle with guests. Find out where the designated break areas are, and relax there during breaks. Extended breaks or too many breaks are unfair to the client. Musicians should never make the bandleader have to look for you or wait for you onstage.

- **EQUIPMENT:** Musicians and vocalists are required to bring their own mics, chords, stands, and lights. The band-leader has enough to carry. Vocalists should arrive early, with charts, keys, and song lists ready for the band, on every gig. Singers do not have private conversations on the stage during the set. Refer to: *Gig*, May 1999

- **VOLUME:** Please be careful of the volume at all times, especially during dinner, when people are conversing. Refer to: *Gig*, April 1998, May 1999

- **FOOD:** Remember that the client has to pay extra for meals, so do not complain out loud about what you are offered by the host. Your meals are a gift from the client, not a requirement. If it is going to be a problem, pick up something to eat on the way to the gig.

- **GUESTS:** No one is allowed to bring a guest, wife, girl-friend, mother, brother, etc. to any event unless it is cleared. In most cases the answer should be no! Refer to: Gig, January 1998

- **DRINKING:** Under no circumstances is alcohol to be con-sumed before or during the gig. Be discreet if you bring any soft drinks to the stage, and always clean up your glasses before you leave. It should go without saying that all gigs must be drug free. Refer to: *Gig*, March 1997

Any problems, whether business or personal, should be dealt with ahead of time. If it is necessary to seek the help of your agent, bandleader, or fellow musicians, you should do so. It is important to be consistent and to maintain the best image possible.

PART 3
....
CONCLUSION

And so, here we are, looking at the world through our designer sunglasses. The tint changes very little. The world of entertainment has the same glitz, overnight successes, and excesses that permeate any other world of high risk, high stakes, and quick bucks. And the rules of survival are the same:

- Be prepared! (Where have we heard that before?)

- Treat others as you'd like to be treated! (Sound familiar?)

- Keep your mind and body clean!

- Respect time!

- Use your head!

It doesn't seem as though it would take a book of this nature to inform you of what you could get in Sunday school or any of a thousand self-help seminars. But I hope that this book makes it clear to you how easily the music business (entertainment business) can move you away from some of the basics. To me, well-rounded people from every walk of life share the same qualities. Successful people are aware of some of the basic truths that help them to achieve success in their field. We have heard, first hand, how people who do the same things that we do have overcome obstacles, dealt with problems and issues, and continued their journey in this business. I hope that we can all learn from them.

Photo Credits

Index